The Book of Lostwithiel
has been published
in a Limited Edition
of which this is

Number 128

A list of subscribers
is printed at
the back of the book.

THE BOOK OF LOSTWITHIEL

Fore Street, Lostwithiel 1825; watercolour by G. B. Lawrance. (RF E-C)

A natural place for a settlement to develop; Lostwithiel engraving, 1813.
(DB)

THE BOOK OF LOSTWITHIEL

BY
BARBARA FRASER

BARON
MCMXCIII

PUBLISHED BY BARON BIRCH
FOR QUOTES LIMITED
AND PRODUCED BY KEY COMPOSITION,
SOUTH MIDLANDS LITHOPLATES, CHENEY & SONS LTD,
HILLMAN (PRINTERS) LIMITED AND
WBC BOOKBINDERS LTD

© Barbara Fraser 1993

All rights reserved. No part of this publication may be reproduced, stored in a retrieval system, or transmitted, in any form or by any means, electronic, mechanical, photocopying, recording or otherwise, without the prior permission of Quotes Limited.

Any copy of this book issued by the Publisher as clothbound or as a paperback is sold subject to the condition that it shall not by way of trade or otherwise, be lent, re-sold, hired out or otherwise circulated without the Publisher's prior consent, in any form of binding or cover other than that in which it is published, and without a similar condition including this condition being imposed on a subsequent purchaser.

ISBN 0 86023 502 5

Contents

ACKNOWLEDGEMENTS	8
FOREWORD BY THE MAYOR OF LOSTWITHIEL	9
INTRODUCTION	9
BEFORE LOSTWITHIEL	10
A PLANT OF EXOTIC GROWTH	15
THE EARLS' FAIR CITY	22
THE BLACK PRINCE	29
DECLINE AND DEVELOPMENT	33
THE CIVIL WAR	42
POWER AND INFLUENCE	50
INTO THE 19TH CENTURY	65
THE VICTORIAN ERA	73
WITHIN LIVING MEMORY	85
HERE AND NOW	118
BIBLIOGRAPHY	126
INDEX	128
SUBSCRIBERS	131

Acknowledgements

My thanks go to the Mayor and Town Council of Lostwithiel for their support, and to all the people who have helped me to prepare this book by giving freely of their time to talk to me. I am also grateful to Jefferys of Fore Street, Lostwithiel, for their generosity in sponsoring the project, in particular to John Keast for his support, and members of staff at the Lostwithiel office, who have dealt with all the typing and photocopying.

I am indebted to the late Mr John Keast of Looe, whose notes were made available to me, and to Donald Dunkley, who has made a lifetime study of Lostwithiel, and generously shared his konwledge with me.

My thanks also go to the Town Clerk, Fran Denison, and to Sally Whiffing and Colin Buck for all their practical help, and time spent in discussion, which has been invaluable.

I thank the staffs of those branches of the County Library who have dealt with the subscriptions for the book, especially Rosemary Kerr and Janet Simon of Lostwithiel Branch, for all their help.

I am grateful for the help given by the staffs of the British Library, the British Museum, the Royal Archives, Windsor, Cornwall County Records Office, the County Archaeology Unit, the Royal Institution of Cornwall Library, the Cornish Studies Library, the Institute of Cornish Studies, the National Trust, Plymouth Museum and Art Gallery and the Royal Naval College Library, Dartmouth.

I thank Jonathan Barker, photographer of Lostwithiel and Ian Fraser, who have done most of the photographic work, also Cyril Bunn and Margery Worden of Lostwithiel, who have contributed their work.

The following kindly gave permission to reproduce material: *Ptolemy's Map of Britain,* Ref Maps c.1.d.3, copyright British Library; *Edward I returning from Gascony,* from a 15th century Flemish manuscript, Ref MSS No ROY 15EN, copyright British Library; *The Caneing in Conduit St* Ref 8826, copyright British Museum; the Royal Archives, Windsor, the National Trust, the Cornwall Records Office, the Cornwall Archaeology Unit, the Cornwall Archaeological Society, the Royal Institution of Cornwall, the Cornish Studies Library, the Devon and Cornwall Record Society; The Lostwithiel Town Council, the Lostwithiel Museum, Lostwithiel Social Club, the Rector and PCC St Bartholomew's Parish Church; Christine Barnicoat, Jonathan Barker, Jill Blanchard and Michael Olver, Don Breckon, Ron and Doreen Brown, Daphne Bryant, Cyril Bunn, Richard F. Edward-Collins, Charles Day, Ian Fraser, Capt J. Desmond, G. Fortescue, Margaret Hoskins and Pauline Dustow, Margaret Hurrell, Jefferys of Lostwithiel, Rosemary Kerr, Ian and Carol Kitt, Doris Liddicoat, Victor and Angela May, Bruce and Florence Netherton, Warren Nicholls, Ryan Rowe, Malah Rundle, M. Eileen Shimmins, June Stephens and Joy Worden, Rev F. Sydenham, Desmond and Eileen Talling, Amy Tanner, Desmond Trethewey, Margery Worden.

Finally, thank you to Ian for all his help and encouragement.

Dedication
For my grandchildren,
Matilda, Florence, Miriam,
Elanor, Lewis, Luca and Natasha.

Foreword

by A. Warren Nicholls, Mayor of Lostwithiel

It is over 100 years since the last full length book was written about Lostwithiel, so it gives me great pleasure to be writing this foreword to *The Book of Lostwithiel* during my term of office.

This small Cornish town, which owes its existence to the River Fowey, has a long and fascinating history, which can be found in its ancient buildings and in the surrounding countryside. As Mayor I find myself part of that history, one of the long line of men and women who have held this office since at least 1290. In that year Serlo Oneynte was Mayor; his name is engraved on a link of the Mayoral chain.

In this book Barbara Fraser presents a panorama of the town from its beginnings to the present day, and brings it to life for us. I am pleased to recommend the book to you.

Introduction

When I was invited to write this book, it was described in the local press as 'a daunting task for Barbara'. So it was! But it has proved to be an exciting challenge, totally engrossing, and made thoroughly enjoyable by the warmth of the support I have received, for which I am most grateful, and I thank all the many people of the town who have helped me.

The town is so rich in history that it has been impossible to include everything in a book of this nature. I have aimed to cover the important developments over 900 years, and to recall some incidents and characters from the past and the present.

I apologise for any omissions and mistakes; I have done my best to find the truth, and have indicated where there can only be conjecture and speculation. During the Civil War many local records and documents were destroyed; other have been lost since. These, alas, are gone for ever. There has been little archaeological investigation in Lostwithiel and Restormel Castle to uncover evidence of the early history. This is waiting to be done, and will be an exciting project one day.

I feel privileged to live here. Whether we were born here or choose to live here we, who love Lostwithiel, respect and cherish its history, and we all carry some responsibility for its present and its future.

ABOVE: Below the town the river meanders through water meadows
... (IF) BELOW: ... then flows through richly wooded country to the
sea. Watercolour by Lawrance. (RFE-C)

Before Lostwithiel

From any of the hills surrounding Lostwithiel one can look down on this compact little town nestling in the valley of the River Fowey, and marvel at the beauty of its situation.

About 100 years ago Arthur H. Norway, in his *Highways and Byways of Devon and Cornwall* described this area as being 'the loveliest inland scenery in Cornwall'.

Quite apart from its beauty it is clear that here was a natural place for a settlement to develop. It stands at the upper tidal reach of the river, 6½ miles inland from the estuary. The river was once navigable by seagoing ships, although it was fordable at low tide. The valley, narrow higher upstream, opens out to provide a small area of level land, protected on all sides by well-wooded hills. Below the confluence with the small tributary stream, the Cober (which now runs under South Street in a culvert) the river meanders through water meadows and on through richly wooded country to the sea. It was after the Norman Conquest, when the barons built their castle at Restormel, that Lostwithiel came into being as a town, planned and developed by private patronage.

It is still a small town, having a population of about 2,600, in the Eastern division of the Hundred of Powder.

In these surrounding hills there is evidence of human habitation going back at least 3,000 years. There are tumuli at Boconnoc, the burial grounds of Bronze Age people, who lived in hill settlements. Merchants from the Mediterranean are thought to have come to Cornwall to trade in those far-off days. It is likely that the river was already being put to good use, both for transport and as a source of food.

Castle Dore, on the west bank of the river between Lostwithiel and the estuary, is the best local example of Iron Age occupation. Ralegh Radford in the 20th century wrote that 'The fortified village can only have contained a small community not exceeding 150 ... It flourished during the 1st century AD but did not survive to the end of that century'.

The 18th century historian Borlase believed that there were two Roman roads into Cornwall from Exeter — one passing via Stratton to Bodmin, and a southerly road by way of Horsebridge, the Hurlers and Braddock Down, fording the river below Lostwithiel *en route* west. F. M. Hext (1891) recalled that workmen cutting a canal at Pontsmill in the 19th century, 'laid open the arched work of a bridge and a road of Roman construction' which would support this theory. Borlase mentioned 'a stone causeway between Lostwithiel and Bodmin, the remains of which existed about midway between the two towns, and which tradition ascribed to the Romans'.

The Giants Hedge, parts of which remain, may have been a Roman road, although some historians believe it was a later defensive earthwork. Extending from Looe to Lerryn it was in parts seven feet high and 20 ft wide and had a ditch on either side. Roman coins have been found at Lerryn.

The Romans maintained several small forts in Cornwall from which officials kept an eye on the tin trade. The Roman settlement at Nanstallon, Bodmin is thought to have been occupied for about 25 years; Bodmin was the centre of the early tin industry. Aerial photographs of a spur above Restormel Castle, taken in 1968 (for English Clays Lovering Pochin & Co Ltd) revealed an earthwork consisting of three concentric rectangular enclosures with rounded corners. The inner enclosure measures 77 x 64 metres. This is believed to be a Pre-Roman hill fort, which would have been occupied into the Romano-British period. Scraps of Roman pottery have been found in the area. It is likely that tin from Bodmin was shipped to the coast from Restormel in those days, (there is evidence that the river was navigable that far, and that there was a quay). It is conceivable that the Romans used the hill fort as a base from which to oversee operations. Perhaps one day more will be known about it.

After the Romans left Britain, around 400 AD, there began a period known as the Dark Ages. Legends flourished, kept alive through the centuries by troubadours and minstrels. The legends of King Arthur have long been associated with Cornwall, most often with Tintagel, but this area may have a claim to be connected with the birth of King Arthur.

Castle Dore was reoccuplied in the 5th century and developed into a palace, which may have been the Castle of Gorlois. Gorlois was a Cornish king married to Igraine. The legends tell that Uther Pendragon fell in love with Igraine and pursued her to her home. There followed the murder of Gorlois and the seduction of Igraine by Pendragon. This was the begetting of Arthur. Might it all have happened so near to Lostwithiel? Another legend told down the centuries was that of Tristan and Isolda. This story is believed by many to have been set at Lantyan. Castle in the valley may have been the site of King Mark's palace. There are woods by the river known as Tristan's Woods, where the lovers might have kept their secret trysts.

Another theory is that Castle Dore was the site of King Mark's palace. A stone now standing beside the road into Fowey is inscribed 'DRYSTANS HIC IACET CUNOMARIS FILIUS'. It is said that this 6th century stone records the death of Tristan, son of Mark. Old manuscripts tell of King Mark attending the Church of St Sampson (at Golant) with his Queen (Isolda), mentioning that the Queen gave her best dress to the Church, which was displayed on feast days.

During the Dark Ages Britain was invaded and settled by adventuring hordes from Europe. The Celts in Cornwall constantly resisted invasion and held out against the Saxons until well into the 9th century. It was another 100 years before the Saxon King Athelstan finally controlled the whole of the peninsula. As the Saxons penetrated Cornwall they developed the manorial system, superseding the Celtic way of life. The Celts had organised the land into parishes and lived and farmed independently in scattered hamlets. The hamlet surrounding the Parish Church was known as Churchtown, as Lanlivery Churchtown still is.

The Saxon lord of the manor claimed ownership of the land and most of the inhabitants, and took responsibility for their safety. The men on the manor worked for their lord and farmed small plots for themselves. The original scattered Celtic smallholdings obviated the need for a strip system as used elsewhere in England. The priest farmed his glebe (allotment of land) in return for his services. The reeve acted as magistrate representing the people, and justice was seen to be done. Before 1066 there was an important manor in the Parish of Lanlivery, west of the River Fowey, probably including the land where Restormel Castle and Lostwithiel now stand.

The river was much wider then and its course was further west. The first solid ground was probably where the Church now stands and it is likely that the river was forded, where the bridge now is. If there was a Celtic chapel or a hermitage on the river crossing, as tradition suggests, it was most likely on the same site as the present Church. There were probably homesteads in the valley, belonging to the Manor, a quay and a number of tracks leading off into the hills. The Saxon Lord's name was Grim and his manor was known as Bodarther or Bodardle.

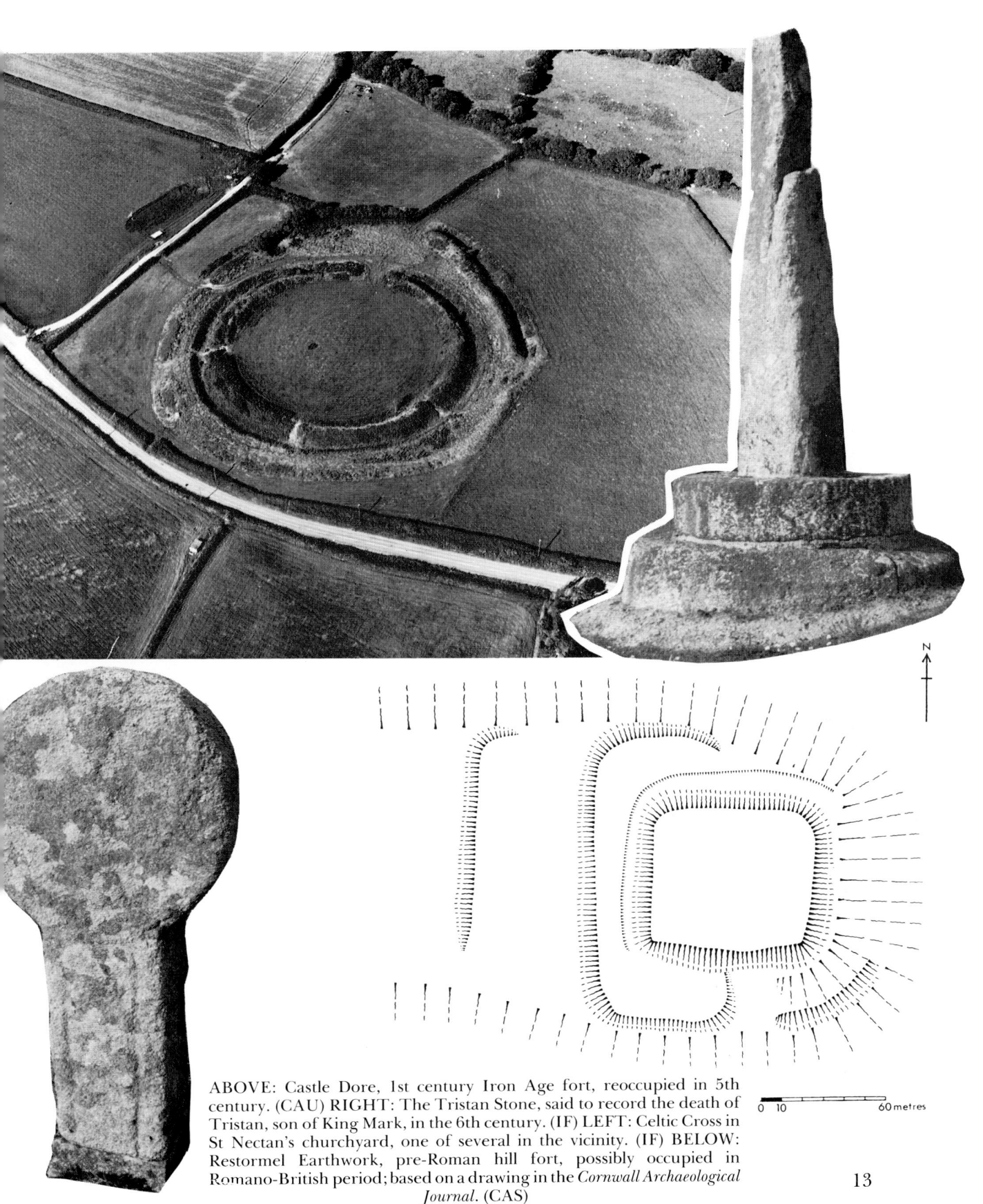

ABOVE: Castle Dore, 1st century Iron Age fort, reoccupied in 5th century. (CAU) RIGHT: The Tristan Stone, said to record the death of Tristan, son of King Mark, in the 6th century. (IF) LEFT: Celtic Cross in St Nectan's churchyard, one of several in the vicinity. (IF) BELOW: Restormel Earthwork, pre-Roman hill fort, possibly occupied in Romano-British period; based on a drawing in the *Cornwall Archaeological Journal*. (CAS)

ABOVE: Restormel Castle; print by S. & N. Buck, 1734. (DB) BELOW: All that remains of Cardinham Castle, probably neglected after the family inherited Restormel. (CAU)

A Plant of Exotic Growth

After 1066 William I subjugated the land. He rewarded loyal knights by giving them each an area to govern. These knights usurped the Saxon lords, taking over important manors, and building castles as a show of strength. Castles were built quickly, in the first instance with wooden keeps. Cathedrals, abbeys and priories were built — with Norman clergy. Thus William dominated Church and State.

In 1086 a census was undertaken throughout the land and details recorded in the Domesday Book. At that time there was no Lostwithiel but the Manor of Bordardle was recorded. (There is still a Bodardle Farm, towards the top of Bodmin Hill). William had given lands in Cornwall to his half-brother Count Robert Mortain, creating him Earl of Cornwall. In 1086 Bodardle Manor belonged to Robert Mortain, and was held for Mortain by Turstin, one of three powerful barons in Cornwall, who held many manors. It was recorded that Grim had paid tax for one virgate of land at Bodardle (a varying measure). There was, however, one hide (sufficient land to support one free family and dependants, usually up to 120 acres). As acres were not the same then as now, it is difficult to estimate how extensive the Manor was.

There was land enough to utilise eight ploughs, each plough needing a team of eight oxen, but there were only four ploughs. There were seven serfs (slaves with no rights), ten villeins (men bound to the manor, who could only attain freedom if they ran away, and remained free for a year and day) and 24 bordars (small holders who paid their rent by labouring). The manor included 20 acres of woodland, 30 acres of pasture, two cobs, one bull and 17 sheep. Bodardle had formerly been valued at 35s and was now worth 20s.

From this manor, Lostwithiel was born. Unrecorded until 1189, or thereabouts, the town came into being at some time between 1086 and 1189. It must have been developed by the Norman lords, after they had established themselves in the manor and begun to build Restormel Castle on a spur commanding the river. It is probable that Baldwin Fitz Turstin, son of Turstin, Lord of Bodardle, started the Castle before the end of the 11th century, The earliest construction was a circular earthwork, with a quadrangular bailey to the west. Baldwin's original keep was probably built of wood, to be rebuilt later in stone. A bridge over the river below the Castle was known as Baldwin's Bridge; here also was a chapel or hermitage dedicted to the Holy Trinity, and a quay. At about that time the Cardinham family was building a castle five miles north east of Restormel. The Cardinhams are said to have descended from Bertrand de Dinant, one of two brothers, who accompanied William I to England. The descendants of Turstin and Bertrand married, joining the two estates, and the Cardinhams took over Restormel.

At that time Devon and Cornwall were the only sources of tin known to the western world, and there was great demand from London and throughout Europe. Bodmin was still the centre of the industry in Cornwall, and the main market for refined tin. The Norman lords would not fail to see the great opportunities that a town here could afford. The River Fowey, navigable by seagoing vessels, made this an obvious port for Bodmin. So, most probably, the town was conceived and developed as a commercial venture. Many workers would be needed, craftsmen in wood, stone, metal and leather, and labourers to fell trees, quarry stones and transport material, more men that Bodardle could provide. It is likely that craftsmen came over from Brittany, and maybe some labourers were escaped villeins. At all events, there must have been a great influx of people and surge of activity over a number of years to establish a new town, 'A Plant of Exotic Growth' as Charles Henderson (1935) was to describe it. The first buildings were probably temporary wooden constructions followed, as the town was established, by more permanent stone buildings. At some time during the 12th century it acquired the name *Lostwetall* or *Lostwidiel*. It was also known as *The port of Fawi* together with the other small ports, Golant, Bodinnick and Polruan (for Fowey did not then exist).

A regular tin route developed from here to Oléron, an island in the Bay of Biscay. From Oléron tin was distributed to La Rochelle, Bayonne and Bordeaux, and was also shipped to the Mediterranean — to Barcelona, Genoa, Messina and the Levant.

Soon after the Norman Conquest, a Benedictine priory had been set up at Tywardreath. St Andrew's was a daughter priory to SS Sergius and Bacchus, at Angers in France. The Cardinhams, now patrons of this 'alien' priory and of Lanlivery Church, built a daughter church in their new town. This was in honour of St Bartholomew, the patron saint of tanners. The tanning industry went alongside the smelting of tin, as it used the bark from the trees felled for charcoal. It is likely that there were local tanneries in those early days.

The design of the church, with its lean-to aisles, was common in Britanny (although there were only two in Cornwall) indicating a strong Breton influence. The recesses found in the west end of the south wall are said to have been intended for the tombs of Robert Cardinham and his wife. Stories vary as to whether or not human remains were ever found there.

The Church may have had links with the Crusades in the 12th and 13th centuries, situated as it was at the point of departure for Mediterranean lands. Crusaders from the West Country may have kept vigil at St Bartholomew's Church, before setting out to fight the infidel.

Almost certainly the street layout of the town was deliberately planned. This planning was not unique, for other 'new towns' in Britain and in France were developed in a similar way at about the same time. The land configuration favoured the grid pattern of Lostwithiel, the Fowey running north to south, and the Cober forming the southern boundary, coming in from the west. The east-west lie of the Church fitted neatly into the scheme. However, a lane must have run north-south immediately west of the Church for, when a tower was added some time later, a right of way continued through it. This remained in use throughout the centuries until the 1870s.

By 1186, Robert Cardinham, Lord of Bodardle, Restormel and Cardinham, had inherited through his wife 71 knights' fees, about 42,000 acres of land between the river and Tywardreath, all the Waters of Fawi from the Haven to Respryn 'where 2 oxen yoked together could walk in the river bed'. Robert was now rich and powerful indeed, he had developed his castle, the Church had been established in the town, the river bridged, a quay for seagoing ships was in regular use, and Lostwithiel was becoming a thriving commercial asset. It now needed a market. Robert applied to the King for permission to establish one, paying 10 marks for the privilege. Now was the time to keep the townspeople content by reiterating their rights and privileges and increasing their opportunities for trade. Robert granted a charter to the town in which he referred to a previous charter, of which there is no record.

Robert's charter, undated, but calculated to have been around 1189, is the earliest surviving document including Lostwithiel, and giving it a name.

'Know all ye, as well present as to come, that I, Robert de Cardinham, here given and granted and by this present Charter have confirmed to all my Burgesses and men of

Lostwithiel, and to all those who hold burgage, tenements or land in the same town, all honours, liberties, dignities and quittances (as far as I can for myself and my heirs) which my ancestors gave them of old on the day on which they founded the town — To wit — every Burgess shall hold his burgage, tenement or tenements hereditarily by rendering for each burgage sixpence annually — To wit — threepence at Easter and the same number at the Feast of St. Michael in discharge of all services and demands.

'And at his death his testament shall be valid, but his heirs shall for a relief of twelve pence hold his hereditaments freely and hereditarily and possess them in peace. Moreover the aforesaid Burgesses and men of the aforesaid town and their heirs, shall remain free and quit of all sullages and customs by land and sea.

'And if by chance any one of them shall be impleaded he shall answer before me or my bailiffs in the said town of Lostwithiel, freely without cause or motion, and not elsewhere. And if he shall incur a fine he shall be quit for sixpence.

'And if he shall be convicted of blood or wounds he shall give security for twenty pence and pay them as shall be mercifully allowed him by me or my bailiffs.

'And if I shall wish to make a Provost, the aforesaid Burgesses shall elect from those perons who are resident in the often hereinbefore mentioned town. Moreover, it is to be noted that the above-named Burgesses may give their sons, daughters and kinsfolk in marriage, without licence or suit, whensoever and to whomsoever they will. But no stranger shall keep a shop out of a ship, that is to say, in the town, except by the permission of the Provost and the whole Townsfolk.

'And if any Burgess should wish to sell his burgage tenement, he may do it without suit save my right — To wit — twelve pence from the purchaser (through my favour or that or my bailiffs).

'Likewise if any of the oftentimes named Burgesses shall have any tenant in the said town of Lostwithiel, he may freely and fully hold a court for him.

'That this may remain ratified and unshaken for the time to come I have strengthened it as well by the testimony of this present writing as by the affixing of my seal.'

The witnesses were John, son of Robert, then steward; Richard, Stephen and Roger, sons of Robert; Richard of Pencoid, Otho of Penpol, and many others.

The privileges granted to the men of Lostwithiel, to be free men, to have hereditary rights over property, and to elect a Provost (mayor), show how town life was progressing.

So fast was foreign trade developing that a few years on, in 1203-1205, the returns of Winchester Assize Hall refer to the *Port of Fawi* as the thirteenth port of the realm, out of a total of thirty-five, for the value of foreign trade, excluding tin (which was exempt from subsidy). If the value of tin had been included, Lostwithiel would have held seventh place. Its foreign trade was greater than all the Cinque Ports together, and it was second only to Southampton on the south coast. Exports included tin, wool, fish and timber. Foreign ships brought goods to the town, which they sold from their decks.

From the mid-12th century miners developed rights and freedoms, particularly the right of 'bounding', whereby a man might search for tin on any land. If he staked out his claim and registered it lawfully, he was free to keep the tin he found. There was no formal administration of the Stannaries (tin mining districts) except the collection of taxes for the Crown. In 1198 the King appointed a warden, De Wrotham, to organise the trading in tin; King John granted a charter to the miners in 1201 confirming their rights of bounding. Stannary Courts were established at about that time.

How and when the town acquired its name is a mystery, about which there are many theories. The name was spelt *Lostwetell* in 1189 and also *Lostwidiel*, but over the years there have been many more variations. The early 17th century historian Camden claimed that the town was the *Uzella* of Ptolemy's map (Ptolemy was a Greek scholar and cartographer of the 2nd century AD) and that it stood originally near to the site of Restormel Castle. Camden thought that *Les Uchel* (*Lofty Place*) and *Uzella* were the same place. If the Romans occupied the hill fort above Restormel before the mid-2nd century, perhaps this was *Uzella* or *Les Uchel*; maybe the name of the Norman town was derived from this. (The fort was identified as *Uzella* on the first OS map, 1813.)

Carew, in the 17th century, thought the name came from two Cornish words: *Lost,* a tail, with *Withiel,* a lion. He suggested the town was the tail of the 'lion' in the Castle. A more likely translation is from the Old Cornish *Lostgwdeyel* meaning 'tail' and 'wooded area' thus coming to mean 'the place at the end of the wood'.

Robert Cardinham was succeeded by his son Andrew between 1224-27, and at Andrew's death Restormel and Lostwithiel were passed to his daughter Isolda, who later married Thomas de Tracy of Barnstaple. The Prior of Tywardreath held the estates for some time, probably in trust during Isolda's minority. In 1264 during the war between Henry III and the barons, Sir Thomas de Tracy signed a warrant to deliver the Castle to Simon de Montfort, who had taken up the barons' cause. This came to nothing, as Simon was killed soon afterwards at the battle of Evesham.

In 1268, possibly on the death of her husband, Isolda granted part of Bodardle Manor 'to the East of the Via Regia which runs from Bodmin to Lostwithiel' together with Restormel Castle and its park, to Richard, Earl of Cornwall.

A collection of deeds of this time, known as the *Cartulary of Earl Edmund*, shows that shortly after that, Richard was granted 'the whole town of Lostwithiel, and the water of Fowey', and later, that part of Bodardle Manor known as Penknek. With the property went 'Villeinage in desmene' — no freedom yet for the villeins.

12th & 13th century 'tin route' from the *Port of Fawi*. (IF)

LEFT: St Bartholomew's Church, showing lean-to aisles, a 12th century Breton design. (IF) RIGHT: Recesses in the south wall of the church, said to have been intended as tombs for Robert Cardinham and his wife. (IF) BELOW: The Martyrdom of St Bartholomew — remains of a painted alabaster carving in the Church, rediscovered and restored, 1839, (SBC). (IF)

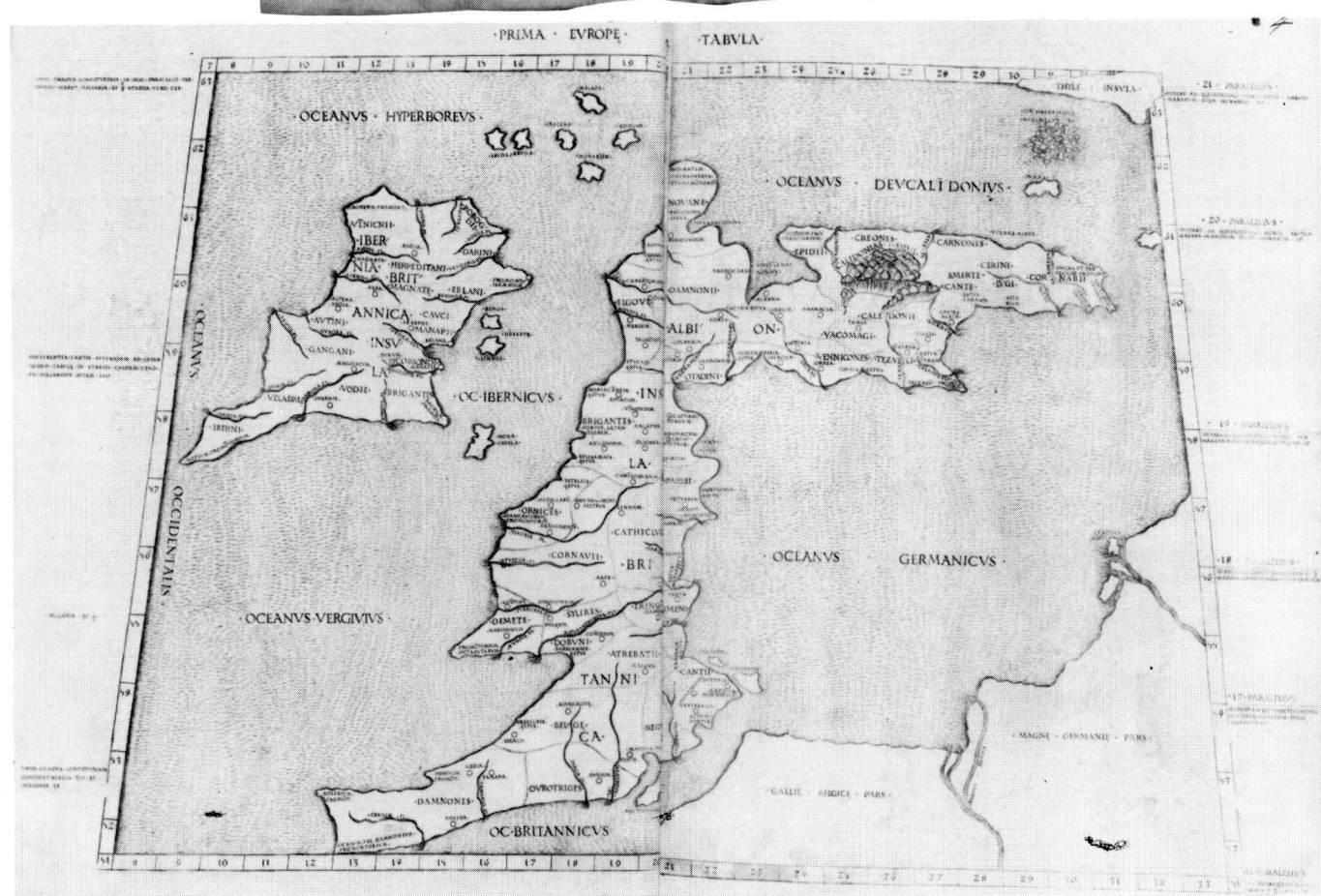

ABOVE: Robert Cardinham's charter, c1189. (CRO) BELOW: Ptolemy's map of Britain, showing Uzella, west of the Tamar; was this the hill fort at Restormel? (BM)

Castle and town: *Lostgwdeyel* 'at the tail of the wood'? (CAU)

ABOVE: Copy of the charter of Richard, Earl of Cornwall, 1269. (CRO)
BELOW: 18th century engraving of Shire Hall, in ruins after the Civil War, the river Cober flowing under the archway into the river Fowey. (DB)

The Earls' Fair City

Richard, Earl of Cornwall, born in 1209, was already approaching sixty years of age when he received the lands from Isolda de Tracy. He was the son of King John, the younger brother of King Henry III. He went on a crusade at an early age, and was granted the Earldom of Cornwall when he was 22 years old. As such he received dues on all the tin mined in the County. Richard was a good businessman and grew to be possibly the richest man in the realm, owning land and castles throughout England.

Richard supervised and financed the re-coinage of the country, keeping a proportion of the profits. He had many Jewish friends and business associates, some of whom were probably involved in the tin industry in Cornwall. Jews were involved in smelting from the 12th century. The smelting furnaces near the mines, in the early days, were known as Jews' Houses.

As Regent in 1254, Richard summoned the first full assembly of elected Knights from the Shires. This can be seen as an early model for Parliament. Although it failed, it was an important landmark, and the precedent was not lost. Richard's biographer Denholm Young (1947) claims that he had 'a real but not always acknowledged place in the history of Parliament'.

Negotiatons began in 1256 to make Richard King of the Romans. The title was granted by seven princely and ecclesiastic electors in Germany; it cost Richard a total of 28,000 marks. He was crowned at Aachen in great splendour by the Bishop of Cologne in 1257. Richard's reign as King of the Romans lasted fifteen years, only three years and nine months of which he spent in Germany.

He was involved in the war with the barons, taken prisoner at the Battle of Lewes in May 1264, and held in the Tower of London until September 1265. The *Melrose Chronicle* says his release cost £17,000 sterling, in addition to £5,000 of 'desirable gold'. Richard gave many years of loyal support to his weaker brother, Henry III.

This then was the man who, although already owning Tintagel, Trematon and Launceston Castles, sought to acquire Restormel and Lostwithiel. Richard no doubt saw the advantages of developing the thriving port into a trading centre for tin, and establishing it as the county town.

Soon after acquiring the town, Richard granted a charter dated 13 July 1269, extending the rights of the Burgesses. A copy is preserved among records in the Tower, though the original is nowhere to be found.

'We, Richard, by the grace of God, King of the Romans, always Augustus have granted, and by this present Charter have confirmed to our Burgesses of Lostwithiel and Penknek in Cornwall, that our said boroughs of Lostwithiel and of Penknek be one borough, and that our Burgesses may have there a Guild Mercatory and free and civil customs and Sake and Soke, and Thol and Thegn and Infangenethof: we have also granted them for ourselves and our heirs, that all the said Burgesses be quit throughout all Cornwall, from giving toll in fairs, and in markets, and wheresoever they shall buy and sell, and from pontage, passage, lastage, tollage and stallage. We have granted unto them also that they shall not be impleaded in the Hundred or County Courts, nor on any summons go to please anywhere without their borough of Lostwithiel and Penknek of any plea except pleas to the Crown of the Lord, the King of England belonging, which nevertheless are to be bound over by the same Burgesses until the coming of the Justices. We have granted to them also that they have once a year a fair in their borough. To wit — on the eve, on the day, and on the morrow, of St. Bartholomew — and a market in each week, and they they take distress for their money due, and not paid from their debtors. In testimony whereof we have caused our seal to be affixed to this present writing. These being our witnesses — Robert de Esthall, Archdeacon of Worcestor, our Clerk, Reginald de Boterill, Philip de Bodrigan, and others.

'Given at Wallingford the thirteenth day of July in the twelfth year of our reign'.

The Merchants Guild enabled the Burgesses to regulate their commercial affairs. By means of *Sake* and *Soke* they were allowed to hold their own Courts, and by *Infangnethof* were given jurisdiction over thieves caught in the Borough. By *Thol* they were bound to pay duty on imports, and by *Thegn*, were allowed the status of freemen and landowners, but were bound to give military service to King or nobles on demand. They were excused from all dues and tolls throughout Cornwall, except those to the Crown, and could not be summoned to courts outside the Borough. The Borough was enlarged to include Penknek (later Penknight) which adjoined Lostwithiel south of the Cober, in the Parish of Lanlivery. Penknek was described as already a Borough so perhaps there was another lost charter relating to Penknek.

Richard brought to Lostwithiel all the administration of the county under the guidance of the Sheriff. He established the County Courts here, transferring them from Launceston around 1268. For a brief period the Assize Courts were held here too, but these were restored to Launceston on payment of a fine. Whether or not Richard stated to build the Great Hall (now often known as the Duchy Palace) is uncertain. He certainly created a need for such a building, but four years after taking over Lostwithiel, he died and was succeeded by his son, Edmund in 1272.

Edmund was a capable statesman, and for three years acted as Prince Regent for his cousin, King Edward I, while the King was in France. Edmund was the Earl of Cornwall for twenty seven years. Lostwithiel became the undisputed capital of the county. It is probable that Earl Edmund built the Great Hall, acquiring the land from local Burgesses. An undated charter in the *Cartulary of Earl Edmund* records that he acquired the house and grounds of one Ralph Wiseman, which occupied the corner at the confluence of the Cober and the Fowey. In 1292 William de London gave to Edmund all rights 'in a certain piece of land on which the steps of the Hall of the . . . Earl have been built'. Two years later Michael Quoyant conveyed to the Earl all his rights in the Great Hall.

The whole complex of buildings erected by Edmund was built along the river, by the quay. It occupied the rectangle of land between Fore Street and the River Cober, and between the Fowey and Church Lane. It was never a palace, but rather an administrative centre for the county, housing in Edmund's time the offices and treasury of the Sheriff and the County Courts. It was also the centre for the Stannaries. Here were the Stannary Court, Exchequer and Convocation Hall, the Coinage Hall, assay buildings, smelting houses and Stannary prison. There was also a strongroom, 'the tynne porch', probably for the storage of tin. There were general security locks, but there is no evidence that the Hall was ever fortified. There was accommodation for officials, for expenditure on 'the auditor's bed' is recorded.

This building became the heart of the county, from which all activity was generated. Here would be found the Sheriff, the Steward, the Receiver (collector of revenue), the Feodary (supervisor of feudal affairs), Havenor (supervisor of maritime affairs) and auditors who kept the accounts, all with their lieutenants and servants. Here were lawyers, judges and court officials.

Lostwithiel was the first coinage town and at times the only one in the county. Here, in the Great Hall, the twice yearly coinage of tin became a ritual. After the first smelting, the tin was moulded into blocks. A corner (coin) was struck off each block, and the quality affirmed (assayed). The block was then weighted and stamped. A record of each block, its weight, owner and duty paid, was kept in triplicate. Tinners brought their tin by packhorse, and the coinage could take from two to ten days. There were regular sittings of the Stannary Courts, and doubtless the Stannary Gaol was rarely empty.

Throughout the year Lostwithiel Quay, *The Port of Fawi*, was the busiest in the county, importing wine, salt, iron, garlic, corn, pitch and dried fruits and exporting cured fish, salted hogs, cheese, cloth and tin. Between 1303-10 Lostwithiel had eight ships of its own bringing wine from Bordeaux.

There were annual fairs and weekly markets, when the 'shoppes' around the Great Hall and along the quay would do a brisk trade. Foreign merchants, seamen, tinners, farmers, Duchy officials, itinerant entertainers, all would be regular visitors. Truly this was the capital of the county. A stone bridge of nine arches was probably built during Edmund's time. The foundations of the four most westerly arches have been uncovered from time to time under North Street, as far as the Globe Inn. The present bridge dates from the 14th or 15th century. The course of the river has changed over the centuries, and the rounded arches of the bridge to the east have been added since.

The tower of St Bartholomew's Church was most probably built by Edmund, and the octagonal lantern added in the 14th century. During Edmund's time Lostwithiel became architecturally, as well as materially rich. It is said that Edmund called the town 'The Lily of the Valley' and 'The Fairest of Small Cities'. He had reason to be proud.

Edmund further developed Restormel Castle. Current investigations suggest that he might possibly have rebuilt much of what was there. The new building included a great hall, solar, kitchen, bed chambers and the chapel. The moat surrounding the keep was 60ft wide and 30ft deep; water was brought from a spring in the hills above, by lead pipes. According to a survey of 1337, the bailey of the castle (now almost obliterated) had its own hall, chapel, chambers, kitchen, offices and stables. These buildings housed the servants and men-at-arms.

Edmund took great pride in his deer park, which extended from Restormel Castle on both sides of the river, and contained about 300 deer. Traditionally the Norman Kings had preserved all hunting rights for themselves. In Cornwall these rights were extended to the Earls. But Henry III, in order to increase his revenue, had sold the sporting rights, and Walter Bronscombe, Bishop of Exeter, had enclosed woodlands on his manors of Lanner and Panton near Wadebridge, creating deer parks.

This angered Edmund, and in 1274 there were violent clashes in the park at Lanner between the Earl's men and the Bishop's men. Master Jordan, a former Archdeacon of Cornwall was 'roughly handled', his horse mutilated, and fences destroyed. The knight who led the assault on the Bishop's park was Sir Thomas de Kancia of Boconnoc. He was excommunicated.

Edmund died childless in 1299 and was buried at Hailes, the Cistercian Abbey in Gloucester founded by his father, where his father and his mother Sanchia were buried before him.

At the time of the Earl's death, there were 305 Burgesses in Lostwithiel. With the exception of Launceston it was the largest of the 'new' medieval towns in Cornwall, and the most important. Edmund was the last Earl to reside at Restormel. There followed an unsettled time for the Earldom. John of Eltham was the last. He died in 1336 without an heir.

While Lostwithiel was enjoying its heyday as capital, and only coinage town in Cornwall, there was much resentment elsewhere. Tinners and merchants clamoured loudly against the costs and time involved in transporting tin from all parts of the county. So in 1305 a charter was granted for the coinage of tin at four more towns: Bodmin, Liskeard, Truro and Helston. It confirmed the rights of bounding, freed tinners from ordinary taxes, confirmed Royal pre-emption and outlined the jurisdiction and responsibilities of the Warden of the Stannaries.

King Edward II was indebted to the Florentine Bardi Society. As a favour to them in 1312, he authorised Genoese merchant Antonio Pisano to visit Cornwall, and buy on his behalf, all the tin coined in the county. Two years later he granted Pisano the Royal pre-emption to buy tin. Pisano used Lostwithiel as his coinage town. He was abusing his privileges, using his own balances for the weighing of tin, paying forty two shillings per thousand weight for it, and selling at seventy two shillings. Tinners complained bitterly. This was so uneconomic for them that their numbers fell from three thousand to five hundred, precipitating a recession. Exports fell, and people could not afford to buy imported goods.

Feelings ran so high that in 1315 Pisano's men were assaulted at Lostwithiel, and the next year the King revoked his grant. It was only a partial victory for the Cornishmen; they got rid of the rascally Pisano, but the King appointed a Steward, Richard de Polhampton, to reside at Lostwithiel. He was to have custody of the stamp and to supervise the coining of the tin, which henceforth must take place only at Lostwithiel.

From 1305 Lostwithiel sent two representatives to Parliament. The county was represented by two 'Knights of the Shire', whose election took place in the Great Hall, (until 1832) bringing more people and excitement into the town.

Under the Stewardship from 1315, Lostwithiel continued to enjoy its status and to grow. In 1337 it was the third wealthiest Borough in the county, after Truro and Bodmin. The number of Burgesses had increased from 305 in 1301, to 391 in 1337, and some of these were rich and powerful. The *Caption of Seisons* 1337 indicates that several Lostwithiel men were leasing land from the Crown. Among them were Gerald Curtoys, who leased five acres at Penlyne and eight burgages (house and surrounding plot of land), and Matthew Coombe, who leased three messuages (house, land and outbuildings) and forty-nine acres.

A situation was developing where almost all holders of land were speculators, rich men who sub-leased, and dominated their non-peasant tenants. There were fewer and fewer peasant tenants, 'villeins' farming land directly controlled by the manor. In 1337 King Edward III sought to reshape the adminsitration of the county and created the Dukedom of Cornwall.

The Shire Hall archway now; the river Cober flows though a culvert beneath the flags. (CPB)

ABOVE: *Edward I returning from Gascony;* ships like these sailed between Lostwithiel, France and Mediterranean ports in the 13th and 14th centuries. (BL) BELOW: The keep of Restormel Castle in 1952. (DB)

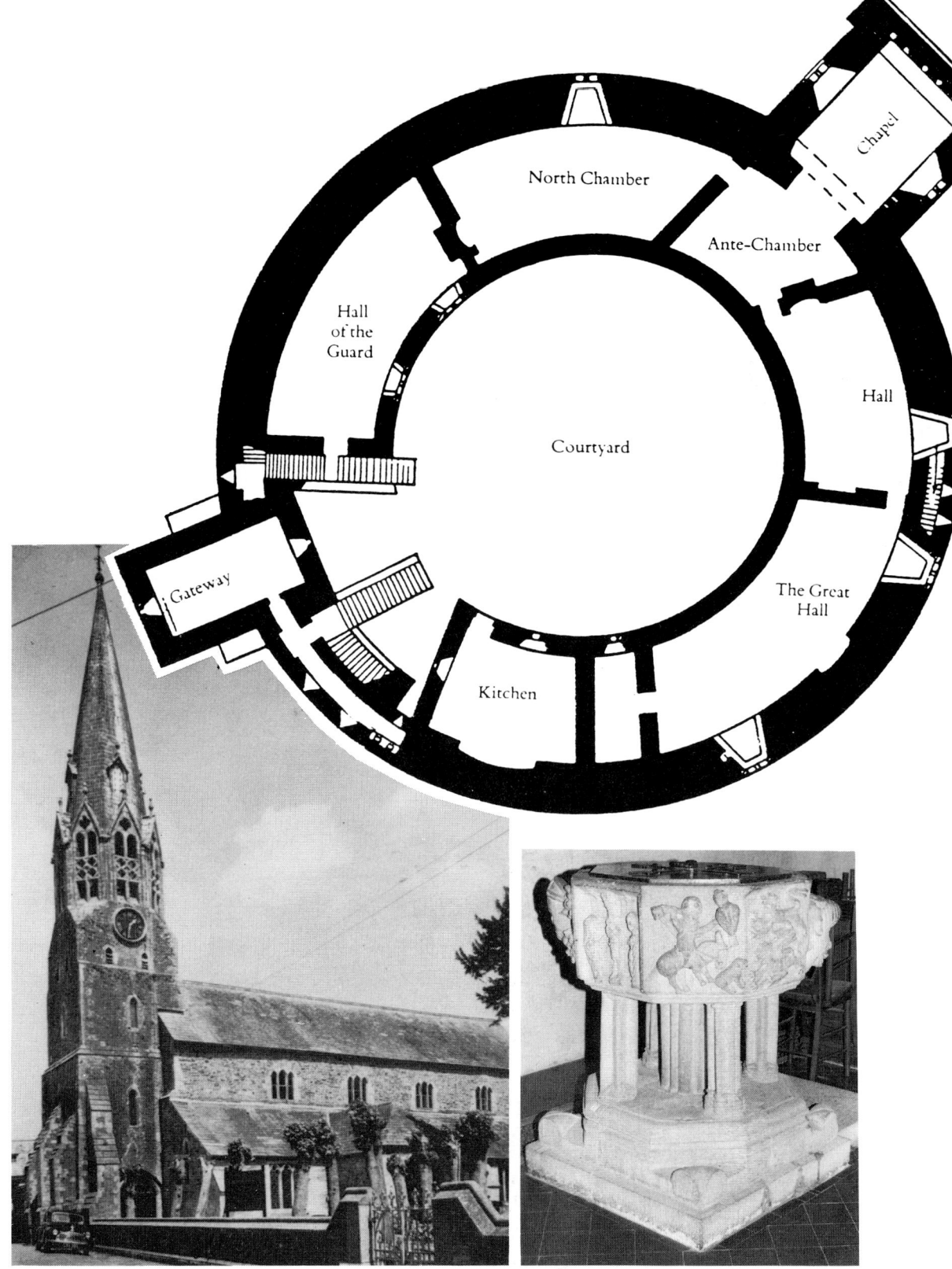

ABOVE: Plan of Restormel Castle keep as it was in Edmund's time. There was also a bailey. LEFT: St Bartholomew's Church tower, probably built by Edmund, the octagonal lantern added in the 14th century. (DB) RIGHT: Octagonal font, 14th century. (SBC) (IF)

The Black Prince

By the 'Great Charter' of 1337, King Edward III created his eldest son, Prince Edward of Woodstock, the first Duke of Cornwall. Prince Edward was then seven years old. He was later known as the Prince of Wales, and nicknamed 'The Black Prince', probably because he wore black armour in battle.

This charter granted to the Duke lands in Cornwall, including Restormel and Lostwithiel. The privileges included the right to appoint the Sheriff of the county, profits of the County and Hundred Courts, and of all ports in the county, including 'wrecks and royal fishes', the rights of prisage and customs of wines, the profits of Stannaries, revenue from Stannary Courts, and the right to take duty on all tin mined in the county, revenues on farms, and baileywicks of Stannaries, and poll tax from tinners working with shovels; also advowsons (right to appoint clergy) of all churches, abbeys and priories. (Cornish possessions formed only part of the Duchy Estates. Other properties were spread across England).

The charter laid down that the Dukedom should be inherited at birth by the first son of the reigning Monarch, and that in the absence of a Duke, the Dukedom should remain in the hands of the Crown.

During the minority of the young Duke, Cornwall was governed from Lostwithiel by a Sheriff and Stewards. The Maritime Court for the county was taken over by the Borough of Lostwithiel, who administered it on behalf of the Crown. It dealt mostly with local cases of poaching, smuggling, rowdysim and disputes in the ports. In 1347 forty-seven ships and eight hundred men from 'Foy Haven' assisted the King at the Seige of Calais. Foy Haven included Lostwithiel, Bodinnick, Polruan, Golant and Fowey. The 800 men no doubt included adventurers and run-away serfs.

The Black Death of 1348-49, carried over Europe by fleas on rats, was probably brought across the Channel by ships, afflicting Dorset and the West Country, and spreading to the rest of England. This pestilence left one third of the tenanted land of Restormel Manor without tenants. Many lessees of the fisheries perished, and no new ones could be found. Overall however, the effects of the Black Death were not so marked in Cornwall as in much of England. The tin mining, fishing and port activities helped to offset the agricultural recession. The size of tenanted farms increased as there was less demand for land, and there was an increase in the amount of sheep rearing, leading to further development of the wool trade. Lostwithiel was an important centre for the collection and export of wool so, having weathered the pestilence, the town gradually recovered.

Prince Edward, Duke of Cornwall, had shown great bravery at the Battle of Crecy, when only 16 years of age, taking the motto 'Ich Dien', 'I Serve'. On coming of age, the Duke set about putting Duchy affairs in order. He was conscious of his position and responsiblities as Duke of Cornwall. *The Black Prince's Register*, a daily log of his orders, shows the attention to detail he brought to his affairs, and gives a clue to the many facets of his personality. Although he gained a reputation for cruelty as a soldier, and was stern in exacting all his Royal dues, he showed concern and compassion for the less privileged of his subjects.

Orders from the Prince were carried by a bailiff-errant, riding from London to Cornwall at least once a week. Sir John Wengfeld was appointed Sheriff, Sir John Dabernoun, Steward, and John de Kendale, Prince's Receiver and Constable of Restormel Castle. The Prince also appointed Brother Robert of the Hermitage of the Holy Trinity, to the Chaplaincy of the Castle for life, to sing Masses for his Royal ancestors.

Sir John Dabernoun was very soon asked searching questions about the administration during the Prince's minority. '. . . enquire how much tin has been forfeited . . . but not answered for, by whom it was forfeited and on what account, into whose hands it has come, and how and for what reasons such forfeitures may fall to the Prince, and to send the inquisition so taken to the Prince between now and the month of Easter next'. Many officials must have been sent scurrying when that arrived.

In July of 1351 the Prince was concerned about 'the repair and safeguarding of the Prince's Castle at Restormel, in this time of war'.

Towards the end of his first year in charge, the Prince enquired particularly about the state of his mills. For ten years the Burgesses of Lostwithiel had leased the mills. They had taken over mill-stones and gear in good condition. Now, it seemed, the machinery was broken and the Burgesses were grinding elsewhere. John de Kendale was instructed to see that the mills were properly repaired at the expense of the Burgesses, and that the Prince's profits were secured.

Eighteen months later the Prince had been reassured that the condition of the mills was due, not to negligence, but to severe deprivation and loss of life during the plague, and he showed his compassion by allowing a 50% reduction in all rents for mills, fisheries and customs for the four years since the pestilence.

He was concerned for his personal effects. He directed four of his top representatives in the county 'to make arrangements amoung themselves for hiring a well manned ship as cheaply as possible . . . to send wines . . . to the Prince at London with speed . . . if . . . there are at sea any special perils . . . they are to put on board the ship, at the Prince's cost, as many archers as they shall think necessary for securing the safe arrival of the wines. They are also to have the tuns . . . well and securely hooped and bunged, so that the Prince may not have so much losss as he had of the wines that were last sent him'. Orders invariably contained the message 'with he least possible cost to the Prince'.

There was constant rivalry between Lostwithiel and Bodmin for the right to sell tin. In June 1353 the Prince ordered the sale of tin to take place at Lostwithiel 'unless too great damage will result to the common people, and especially to the poor tinners, whose estate the Prince would not wish to worsen'.

Early in 1354 Lostwithiel started to prepare for a Royal visit. There were orders from London to repair all defects to castles, manors, houses, bridges and particularly the conduits for the water supply to Restormel Castle. Instructions were received with regard to fuel, food and wine required to cater for the large number of people expected — courtiers, retainers, visiting lords, knights and their servants.

On 20 August 1354 the Prince, preceded by heralds and accompanied by knights and nobles, crossed the newly repaired bridge at Lostwithiel and rode in splendour to establish his court at Restormel. Feudal lords, knights, tenants and burgesses from all over the county came to pay him homage and swear fealty. Among these were John Killigrew of Trematon, also John de Inkepenne from the Manor of Hauton, near Trematon. Inkepenne promised the Prince that, if the castle of Trematon were ever besieged, he would 'be therein with three men armed for the defence thereof, for forty days at his own cost, and forty days at the Prince's cost'.

The burgesses of Helston brought a petition to which the Prince gave his consideration. The friars of Truro paid homage, and were repaid by a promise of ten oaks from the park, suitable for constructing houses, and the friars minor of Bodmin received twenty shillings.

The Court at Restormel lasted for two weeks. By 5 September it had moved on to Launceston. On 11 September orders came for the venison, fish and tin vessels left behind at Restmorel to be sent by sea to Southampton. Lostwithiel must have suffered a great anticlimax after all the months of preparation, and the excitement of the Court.

The Prince made calls on the Duchy to service his wars in France. At one time he called for wine, oats, wheat and brushwood for fires, to provide for eight hundred men-at-arms, waiting to embark at Plymouth. Then he wanted one hundred and four score and eleven sheaves of arrows, also five hundred cod (300 dried, 200 powdered), four hundred salted congers and two hundred salted salmon to be sent to France. Some years later he ordered chargers, trotting horses, palfreys, packhorses and carthorses, eighty altogether, to be sent to Aquitaine, as well as oats and hay to feed them on the voyage. Then in September 1364, four thousand shoes and one hundred and fifty thousand nails were needed in Gascony.

The Prince was impatient with inefficiency, and removed at one stroke six bailiffs from office, ordering John de Kendale to 'put other more able persons in their place'. In 1356 a petition was received from Abraham Lestymour, the tinner, who worked with three hundred men on the moors. He had been assaulted at his mine, by a number of armed officials. On the Sheriff's order he had been imprisoned in Lostwithiel, together with thirty of his servants, until each had paid a 20 shilling fine. Thereafter he had been made to agree to a heavy toll on all tin mined. Abraham asked to be governed in accordance with the tinners' charter.

The problem was that Abraham was streaming tin on moors which were drained by tributaries of the River Fowey. The streaming caused sand and rubble to be carried down into the Fowey, which was rapidly silting up, particularly where it met the tidal flow, interfering with the working of the mills and the fisheries, and making it impossible for seagoing boats to reach the town. Boats of shallower draught had to be used, and much of the tin had to carried by packhorse along rough tracks to small quays downstream. The Prince's instruction was to ascertain the cause of the nuisance. Six months later mining on Redwith and Respryn Moors was discontinued 'as the Prince's mills of Lostwithiel and the Haven of Fowey are well nigh ruined thereby'. All was not well in the blowing house either. There were complaints that pieces of false metal were being inserted into the tin. Offenders were to be dealt with 'in such a manner as shall be a warning to others'.

Almost half of the orders issued to Cornwall were directed to John de Kendale; only on one occasion was there a hint of displeasure with him. This angry outburst must have come as a shock to John: 'The Prince is amazed and moved with anger against him for having shown letters recently sent to him under the Prince's seal, which ought to be kept secret, to those who sued for them; and would have him know that if any fault is found in him again, he will have him chastened that others will take warning from him not to disclose their Lord's counsel in future'.

Nevertheless, eight days later, orders were coming through to John as ever; with never another reference to the misdemeanour.

The Prince visited Restormel Castle on two more occasions. In November 1362 notice came from Plympton 'the Prince intends to come presently to the Castle of Restormel and stay there for Christmas'. Then on board ship in Plymouth Haven in June 1363, he ordered payment to be made to John de Kendale of £12 8s 0d 'which he expended by the Prince's order between St Matthias Day past and Easter following, while the Prince was staying at the Castle of Restormel'.

While the Prince was abroad the Prince's Council managed the Duchy on his behalf. By now the silting of the river was serious indeed, and so the mining of tin which had been the source of Lostwithiel's prosperity and high status, brought about its gradual decline. The Prince, whose health had suffered as a result of his military career, returned to England and died at the early age of forty-six years. Lostwithiel is proud of its association with one of the most respected of medieval princes.

LEFT: The Black Prince, Edward, 1st Duke of Cornwall (1330-76) — as illustrated in an 18th century history book. (IF) BELOW: The emblem of the Black Prince was added to the Shire Hall during his Dukedom. (JB) RIGHT: The bridge originally had nine medieval arches. The remains of the four most westerly ones are under North Street. (LM) BELOW: The remains of a 14th century chapel window in North Street. (MW)

Decline and Development

Following the death of the Black Prince in 1376, Richard II granted the town another charter, confirming the liberties, privileges and responsibilities it already held. Lostwithiel was sometimes referred to as the Royal Borough or *Villa Regis*.

The port had declined, losing its seagoing trade to ports nearer the estuary. Goods to and from Lostwithiel were carried by boats drawing no more than seven feet of water. Lostwithiel retained its rights over the river, and was entitled to dues from all ships using its ports, until the formation of the Fowey Harbour Board in 1870. The Mayor held jurisdiction over the Maritime Courts and, for some time, the title of Admiral of the River. The ancient privilege, which had become a formality by the 17th century, was symbolised by the silver oar given to the town by Silas Titus, MP from 1663-79, who also gave the mace. These are now part of Lostwithiel's civic regalia.

During the 14th century, block houses had been built at Fowey and Polruan, and a protective chain slung between them, to protect the river from French marauders. A hundred years later the men of Fowey Haven were engaging in piracy on their own account, terrorising foreign ships in the Channel and seizing their cargoes.

In 1449 Sir Hugh Courtney of Boconnoc was involved with three others, in seizing a Spanish vessel, sheltering in Plymouth Sound. They put the Spaniards ashore, brought the ship to Fowey and sold off the cargo. This sort of piracy was difficult to control as the local men dispensing justice were mostly involved in piracy themselves. Twenty-five years later this lawlessness still prevailed, and the exasperated King sent his own commissioners to restore order. They arrested all the mariners, masters and victuallers of ships in Fowey, Polraun and Bodinnick, and imprisoned them in Lostwithiel Gaol. They tricked the merchants and burgesses of these towns into coming to Lostwithiel (as they thought on business) where they also were held in custody. Their ships, gear and goods were confiscated. Many dire punishments were meted out, and one Captain Harrington was executed at Lostwithiel. As a final act of retribution, the defensive chain across the harbour was removed, and given instead to Dartmouth. Carew, telling the story, wrote 'their wonted jollity transformed into a sudden misery, from which they strived a long time to relieve themselves'. The gallows at Lostwithiel had been set up by Earl Edmund; tradition has it that the site of this was the small plot of land at the top of Bodmin Hill, known for centuries as Gallows Hill Head.

Throughout most of the 14th and 15th centuries Lostwithiel was still the only coinage town in the county, apart from sharing coinage with Truro for a short time. Sometimes there were four coinages in the year, taking place at Lady Day (March 25), Midsummer (June 21); late August and Michaelmas (September 29) sometimes there were only two.

For centuries there had been a Stannary Parliament or Convocation, which met from time to time in the Great Hall at Lostwithiel. Convocations, called by the Warden, were made up of twenty-four Stannators. Six Stannators were nominated to represent each of the four stannaries, or mining districts, by the Mayor and Burgesses of the four appropriate towns; Launceston, Lostwithiel, Truro and Helston. Lostwithiel chose the Stannators for the Blackmore Stannary, the mining area between Bodmin and St Austell. The business of the Parliament covered all aspects of Stannary affairs.

Throughout the centuries there was constant smuggling. All classes of men used every ingenious method they could devise, to avoid paying duty. Stannary laws were passed at various times to combat this.

Meetings of the Parliament took place in private. It had the power to question any arrangements made by the Duke of Cornwall or the Sovereign, concerning the Stannaries. However, decrees of the Stannary Parliament had to be signed by the Stannators, the Warden and the Duke, in order to become law. So, in effect, the Stannators could be overruled. It is doubtful whether the Stannators really represented all classes of tinners, chosen as they were by Mayors and Burgesses who had an interest in keeping their Duke and his administrators happy. As time went by, mine owners and merchants appeared among them until, by the 18th century, members of the Cornish landed gentry were elected Stannators. In 1674 each Stannator was allowed to choose a non-voting assistant, in order to be kept informed of the opinions of lower class tinners. Soon even assistants were being chosen from the gentry class. The need for a Stannary Parliament gradually diminished and the last one was held in 1752.

The Stannary Courts, controlled by a Steward, assisted by bailiffs and with a jury of tinners, dealt with all legal disputes relating to tin, until coinage was finally abandoned in 1838. During the 16th century the Star Chamber Court of Henry VIII had a right to hear appeals from the Stannary Courts.

Back in the 15th century the Great Hall was still the centre of power in the tin industry; between 1460-70 major repairs to the roof were undertaken. In 1496, by Act of Parliament, Henry VII had new weights and measures made for the county, to be used in Lostwithiel. These are now part of the town's treasure, and are kept in the Mayor's parlour.

Tin had for centuries been bought for the manufacture of pewter, made up of 80%-85% tin, combined with lead or copper. There were always pewterers among the traders buying tin, and there were also pewterers living and working in Lostwithiel in the 17th century. As the production of tin increased in the late 16th and 17th centuries, pewter became more fashionable, and began to replace wood as a material for domestic utensils. The use of pewter tableware indicated a family's social status.

The increase in tin production, however, was in the west of the county and, unfortunately for Lostwithiel, it coincided with a sharp decline in tin produced from Blackmore and Fowey Moor. Miners were moving west to find richer lodes. By the beginning of the 17th century only 15% of tin was produced in the east of the county, and Truro took over from Lostwithiel as the main coinage town.

Lostwithiel merchants, however, were by now investing directly in mines. In 1639 John Haymen of Lostwithiel coined 8% of the total output for the county. Smelters took over as middlemen in the trade, growing rich and becoming part of the developing 'middle class'. Carew writes in 1601 of the wretched living conditions and great poverty of the labourers in the mines, who earned at that time about 8d a day, not enough to house, feed and clothe a family.

During the 15th century the Duchy of Cornwall could be likened to a Palatinate, run like a little state, with its own hierarchy of officials in London, and active administration in Cornwall, largely centred on Lostwithiel.

Life on the manors was still 'unfree' for some, but the feudal system was breaking down; manorial tenants were paying chevage, a fee to the lord of the manor, for permission to live elsewhere. In 1438 there were eight unfree tenants from Stoke Climsland and one from Helstone-in-Trigg living in Lostwithiel.

As the tin industry declined, the wool and tanning industries, and the crafts associated with them, grew in importance. Many poor men had more than one job; some supplemented their income by weaving; their wives and daughters were carders and spinners. Women worked on the farms, in the markets and as servants. Men worked as craftsmen, in the mills, potteries, slaughterhouses and tanneries; they salted and cured meat and fish, loaded and unloaded boats, while others plied their craft up and down the river. Animals were kept by the townspeople in sheds and linneys beside their houses, and grazed on common lands belonging to the town.

In 1490 a dispute arose between the townspeople of Lostwithiel and Richard Curteys of Pill who claimed ownership of two moors beside the river. A rich merchant, Walter Wooley, had given these lands to the Town, they were held in trust, and revenue from them was used for the upkeep of the Church and the bridge. Richard had enclosed about four acres with hedges, enraging the townspeople. They drove their beasts into the enclosure, where they 'did eat up and befoul the grass'. Curteys thereupon impounded the cattle, and proceeded to the Church of St Bartholomew, and announced from there what he had done. It was eventually negotiated that he would release the cattle in return for a promise never to attempt to graze them in the enclosure again. But that was not the end of it, for the Mayor brought an action, in the Star Chamber Court, against Richard.

It is significant that Richard made his announcement from the Church. The Church was central to the life of the town. Throughout the Middle Ages the Church held great spiritual power over the people. At all levels of society there was a great fear of the Lord, as interpreted by priests and prelates. There was superstition mixed with religious beliefs, exacerbated by ignorance.

The Reformation brought both a desire for knowledge and access to it for many more people, which created a new atmosphere and a greater freedom of thought within the Church. This must have had its effect upon the people of the town, once they had overcome the confusion, fear and anger attendant upon the implementation of Henry VIII's Act of Supremacy of 1534. From being a daughter church of Lanlivery, paying revenues to St Andrew's Priory, and owing unquestioned allegiance to the Holy Father in Rome, St Bartholomew's became a Parish Church in its own right, and its congregation was required to recognise the King as Supreme Head of the Church of England. These must have been disturbing times both for the congregation and their first vicar, Peter Waryson, who had been a chantry priest at Liskeard.

About a decade later there was another turbulent period when the medieval chantry of St George, at the eastern end of the south aisle, was dismantled in accordance with the Courts of Augmentation set up by Henry VIII. The chantry had been quite separate from the main church, and had its own priest, John Halwell being the last. Members of the Guild of St George had paid for the upkeep of the chantry, and there were lands belonging to the Guild. There were bitter disputes before the land was confiscated, and the altar stone removed and placed on the floor of the south porch of the Church. It is believed that the marble slab, 7'6" long by 3'1" wide, which lies across the approach to the south porch, is that altar stone, moved into its present position during the 1878 restoration.

Norden in the late 16th century, and Carew in the early 17th, visited Lostwithiel and have described a ceremony which took place each year on Little Easter Sunday, and which was already an ancient custom. Freeholders of the town assembled and chose from among their number, one to be the *Prince*.

Dressed in 'brave apparel', crowned, and carrying a sceptre, the *Prince* was mounted on a horse. Then accompanied by all the others, also on horseback, and with a sword borne before him, he proceeded along the main street to the Church. He was received by the priest wearing his best vestments, at the church gate, and escorted into the Church, together with his attendants, to hear divine service. After the service, the *Prince* and his retinue remounted, and made their way to a house, where a feast had been prepared. Seated at the head of the table, he received homage and acts of fealty from all present, after which they all enjoyed the feast and later returned to their homes.

The original reason for the custom is unknown — perhaps it was to remind the people of their absent Dukes.

There were then twenty-two taverns and inns catering for the needs of townspeople and visitors. Despite all the activity in town, it seems that the growing middle class spent little money on the upkeep of buildings. Leland, making a survey of Cornwall between 1533-40, was appalled at the state of its buildings. In 1540 an Act of Parliament was passed requiring repairs and the rebuilding of derelict houses in several Cornish towns, including Lostwithiel. Apparently nothing was done. Forty-five years later Norden wrote of Lostwithiel 'This town was famous and glorious, but since it was deprived of the Duke's presence it hath lost also her beauty, as appareth by the ruins of many decayed houses'.

The Castle fell into disrepair during the 15th century, Henry VIII disparked Restormel, and stopped the singing of Mass in the Chapel of the Trinity. Leland and Norden wrote of the dilapidation of the Castle, describing it as 'sore defaced', 'now unroofed', 'dissolute', 'foresaken and forlorn'. Carew in 1601 writes of more positive destruction: 'The conduit pipes taken away, the roof made sale of . . . the hewn stones of the windows, durns and clavels pullied out to serve private buildings'.

One wonders whether Taprell House owes anything to the Castle for its great fireplace (there had been one in the bailey) and the squint and granite vaulting in the closet? This impressive Tudor mansion, central to the town, consisted of a great parlour and buttery with chambers above, a malthouse, gatehouse and courtyard. The origins of the house can only be conjectured, for there are no records. Part of the mansion (now the Library and Exhibition Centre) could have been built earlier in the 16th century as a Guild House, and developed later into a dwelling. Parts of the building, now the Dower House, are ancient, and may have been incorporated into the mansion at that time. The house was bought by Richard Mt Edgecumbe in 1742, and belonged to the Edgecombe family until it was sold to Thomas Hoskin in 1911. The town purchased the main part of the mansion, known as Taprell House, in 1934 from Thomas Hoskin, putting it to a variety of uses for 60 years. In 1992 the Council determined to rescue the ancient building from dereliction. It has been sensitively restored under the direction of local architect, John Carter. The project has been funded jointly by the Town Council and the Methodist Church, and the outcome is the subject of justifiable pride. It now houses a Methodist Chapel, a branch of the County Library and exhibition space for the town. The official opening on 1 May 1993 was attended by Taprells from as far afield as the USA and Australia.

The Castle was left to decay, and for centuries it was hidden by trees, shrubs and creepers. Towards the end of the 1920s the Office of Works enclosed the Castle grounds, and started to clear the site and preserve what remained of the building.

In 1946 Bruce Netherton was appointed assistant custodian and, on the retirement of Mr Rowe he became custodian and has been largely responsible for the development of the Castle grounds.

Bruce was awarded the Queen's Silver Jubilee medal in 1977 for his services. He retired in 1986 after giving forty years of loving care to the Castle and its grounds. It is now in the hands of English Heritage. Lostwithiel residents have the privilege of free access to the Castle, for it is by tradition, our refuge in time of danger.

By its charter, Lostwithiel was obliged, in time of need, to muster men and arms for the defence of the realm. In 1569 there were thirty-seven men of Lostwithiel on the Muster Roll; thirteen archers, sixteen bill men (armed with bill hooks), seven harquebusiers (carrying portable guns) and one pikeman. Names on the list included Kendal, Swete, Hellyer, Hendye, Tontyn and Collyns.

Tinners, by their own charters, were exempt from these demands, so in 1588, when there was a real threat of attack by the Spanish, Sir Walter Raleigh, then Lord Leiutenant of Cornwall, Warden of the Stannaries, called a Stannary Parliament at Lostwithiel. By custom, tinners supported the Crown and provided men-at-arms when directed by their own Parliament. As a result of tinners coming forward, and a good response from the towns, Cornwall's Certificate of Musters in 1588 included 5,560 men and an assortment of weapons, ammunition and horses.

Lostwithiel was always one of the less impoverished of Cornish towns, being at the centre of good farming land (although this did not extend very far; 'downend' indicated the extent of the rough downland). In the 15th century there were no officials holding tenancies of Duchy land, a reversal of policy after the death of the Black Prince. As a result there was a growing number of 'yeoman peasants' leasing holdings directly from the manors, and passing them on to their sons when they died.

The appearance of the land was changing. There was a move towards the enclosure of tenant holdings; the high hedges built then are still a feature of the landscape. A form of mixed farming developed, rotating crops and rearing animals. Heavy horses and oxen were used on the land. Some time later Carew noted that these were not well treated, often overworked and too heavily laden. Packhorses and riding horses were the only means of land transport, the tracks unsuitable for wheeled vehicles.

In 1609 a charter of incorporation reorganised the government of the town. There were to be a Mayor, six Capital Burgesses and 17 Assistants (these 24 people were the only ones allowed to vote at elections). There were to be a Recorder (a Borough Magistrate) who held this position for life, and a Court of Record. Courts of 'pye-poudre' were instituted, to be held on market and fair days. These dealt with petty crime 'while the dust was still on the feet'. The population of Lostwithiel at the time was about 900.

The tin coinage hammer and its stamp. (FMH). (RIC)

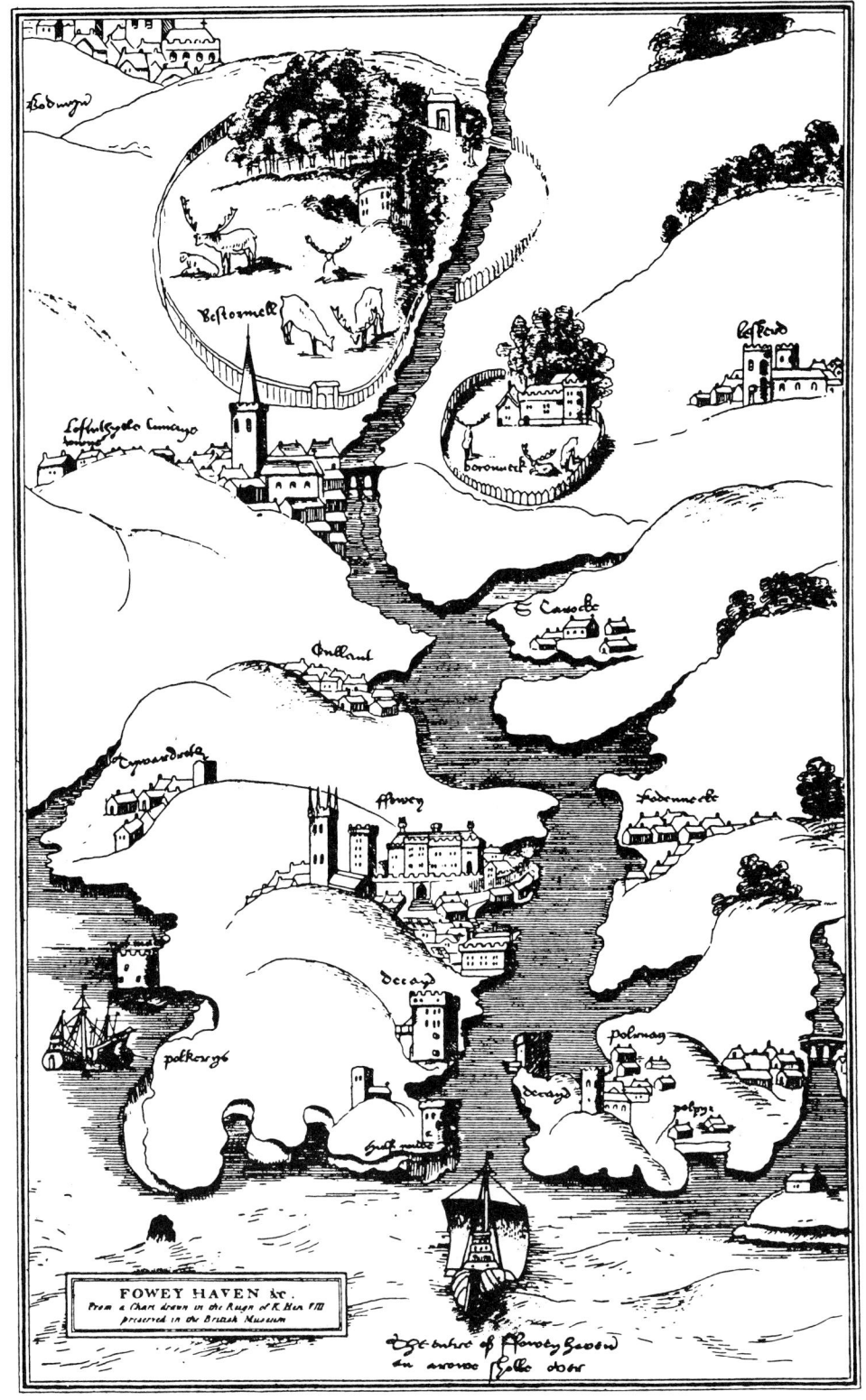

Map of Fowey Haven at the time of Henry VIII from Lyson's *Magna Britannia*. (RIC)

LEFT: Altar stone from St George's Chantry placed as a stepping stone into the south porch of the Church, and the 17th century tomb of the Taprell family. (SBC) (IF) RIGHT: Taprell House, courtyard and east front today. (IF) BELOW: 17th century Cornish emblem on the North gable of the Shire Hall building; an early example. (IF)

ABOVE: Great fireplace, Taprell House, (IF) and CENTRE: upper storey closet, with granite arch and squint-window. (IF) BELOW: Restormel Castle was neglected for many centuries. (DB)

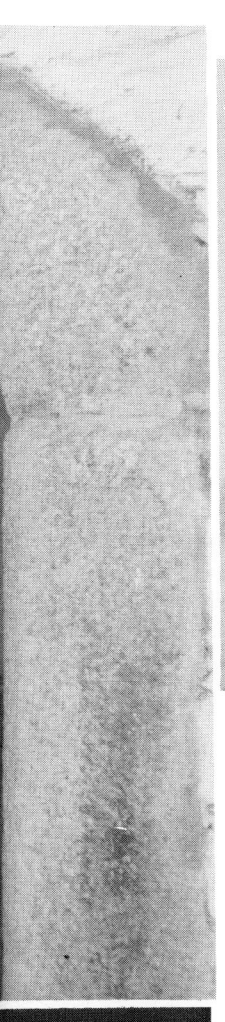

ABOVE: Bruce Netherton received HM the Queen's Silver Jubilee Award in 1977 for services as Curator of the Castle. (B&FM) OPPOSITE and BELOW: Silver mace and oar, given to the town in 1670 by Silas Titus, MP for Lostwithiel. (LTC) (IF) CENTRE: The communion plate — gift of Thomas Jones Esq in 1775 to Mayor, Minister and inhabitants of Lostwithiel. (LTC & SBC) (IF) RIGHT: Silver Seal of Lostwithiel and Penknight, 1735. (LTC) (IF)

LEFT: King Charles I, 1600-1649. (IF) RIGHT: Lord John Robartes, 1st Earl of Radnor, painted by Sir Godfrey Kneller. (NT) BELOW: In the Siege of Lostwithiel, St Nectan's Chapel was caught in the crossfire and lost its tower, which was never replaced. (IF)

The Civil War

The time of England's greatest political upheaval culminated in the execution of the King and eleven years of Commonwealth rule.

Lostwithiel first saw action in January 1643, when Lord Ruthin Gray of the Parliamentary Army marched his men into Cornwall and took up a position on the high ground near to Braddock Church. He expected Lord Stamford to join him with reinforcements.

A smaller Royalist force, including many Cornishmen, waited ready for action near Bodmin. Sir Ralph Hopton wrote in his *Narrative of his Campaign in the West* that, on hearing of the enemy approach, the Royalists 'advanced that night without cannon or baggage to Boconnoc Park'.

Next morning, 19 January, they came upon 'the rebels' at Braddock, and positioned themselves within sight of them on a hill to the west, the valley between them. Hopton was invited to command the troops that day. He arranged his men with the foot in the middle, flanked on each side by horse. Then public prayers were said. The Roundheads, observing this, passed word around that they were saying the Mass.

After prayers, two small brass guns, minion drakes from Boconnoc, were 'speedily and secretly' placed on the left flank. The rebels were still manoeurving their five cannon into position. Hopton fired off the drakes into the midst of the rebel troops, taking them completely by surprise, following up rapidly with a charge of both foot and horse, down the valley and up into the enemy ranks. This put them into utter confusion and disarray. They dropped their arms and scattered, heading off towards Saltash. The Cornish Army took 1,200 prisoners, the five cannon and all the ammunition and arms.

This was the Battle of Braddock Down, a resounding victory for the Royalists, who then chased the rebels out of Cornwall.

For a while life settled down, although there would be soldiers passing through Lostwithiel, and recruiting officers constantly looking for more men.

Lord Robartes of Lanhydrock, a respected Parliamentarian, formed the opinion that the Cornish people would favour Parliament's cause if its Army was here. He succeeded in persuading the Earl of Essex that it would be an easy matter to take Cornwall. Essex, against his better judgement, brought his army of 10,000 men over the Tamar on 20 July 1644. Sir Richard Grenville's army, retreating before him, retired to Truro.

On 2 August, Essex took Lostwithiel and set up his headquarters in the town. He then took Fowey and the harbour, expecting supplies to come from Plymouth. Essex garrisoned the two towns, Restormel Castle, Respryn Bridge and Lanhydrock House, where he himself resided. Thus he held a good central position in the county.

This was the beginning of Lostwithiel's misery. Officers and men, who vastly outnumbered residents, took over the town. Every spare room, parlour, kitchen, linney, every outlying farm, all would be commandeered for the army's use. The soldiers helped themselves to the town's food, and made free in the taverns. There were 2,500 horses to be fed, watered and housed, some of them stabled in the Church.

Essex now summoned the county to rally to Parliament's cause, but everything went badly wrong for him. The King decided to pursue Essex, and crossed into Cornwall, meeting up with Prince Maurice and his army on 31 July.

News that the King was in the county fired the Cornish with Royalist zeal. Richard Symonds, an officer in the King's Army, wrote a diary of the events in August. Grenville moved up towards Bodmin with 800 men as the King advanced with an army of 10,000 foot, 5,000 horse and 28 pieces of cannon.

On 8 August the King set up his headquarters at Boconnoc, and on the 9th Prince Maurice sent a letter to Essex, carried by a trumpeter (said to be Essex's nephew) inviting him to join with the King. Essex replied '. . . I, having no authority to treat without the Parliament who have entrusted me, cannot do it without breach of trust'. There was frequent skirmishing in the hills between Boconnoc and Lostwithiel but no major action.

One day an unusual challenge to battle was received by Col Digby of the Royalist Army, from Col Straughan and a hundred young Roundheads, all between 16-20 years of age. Digby and a similar group of Royalist youths took it up. The protagonists formed up against each other. It is said that Col Straughan led the attack wearing only a hat and a shirt; his young men, however, were well armed for combat. Digby and his youths advanced to meet their adversaries, but fired their pistols before they were within range. Straughan's men then moved in fast, firing among them at close range, killing half of them within minutes, and badly wounding the others. This sad and gratuitous waste of young lives was recorded by three eye witnesses.

Meanwhile, the Royalist armies were closing in on Lostwithiel. The rebel garrison at Respryn abandoned the bridge, leaving free passage between the two Royalist armies. The Royalists took Lanhydrock, giving strict orders that there was to be no plundering. A few days later, a soldier was hanged for disregarding this order. However, it must be told, Robarte's silver was stolen to be melted down in the Royal Mint.

The Royalists took St Austell, Par and St Blazey. The King's army had fortified the eastern bank of the River Fowey. At Hall Walk and Polruan, guns trained on Fowey and the harbour entrance prevented ships from landing. The weather also helped; Cornwall was lashed by cold winds and rain throughout August. The King, inspecting the fortifications at Hall Walk, narrowly escaped death, when a shot from Fowey killed a fisherman within yards of him.

Essex was trapped in Lostwithiel and the Fowey Peninsula. The King's men were foraging as far back as Liskeard for food. For Essex's men it was even worse. The Royalists had scattered papers on the hillsides above Lostwithiel, offering pardon to any rebels who would come over to the King. Many men defected from Essex's army, bringing stories of great hunger.

With all the food in Lostwithiel and the Peninsula gone, and no supplies getting through by sea, everyone was starving, soldiers and civilians alike. The inactivity of the army under these conditions must have driven everyone to desperation, and the violent and destructive behaviour of the soldiers may well have been their reaction to hunger, boredom and incipient fear.

Wilful damage was done to the Church and its valuable records destroyed. Acts of sacrilege took place, such as the christening of a horse at the font, using the name of Charles. The Great Hall was badly damaged and burnt, and lost all its ancient documents. Homes were plundered and the people had no redress. Within three weeks they lost everything, except their anger.

Lostwithiel suffered too at the hands of its friends. On 21 August the Royalists, firing into the town, set the cottages in Bridgend ablaze, at the same time as Grenville surprised and took Restormel Castle. That night the King's men dug a redoubt (gun emplacement) 20 yards square, on a hill overlooking Lostwithiel, from which to bombard the town.

The Patronal Feast Day of the Church of St Bartholomew was 24 August, and on this day the tower and spire were damaged by Royalist cannon fire. It is hard to imagine the effect on parishioners of this 'unkindest cut of all'. They must have despaired.

Essex finally decided to organise an escape. His only option was to attempt to lead the cavalry through the Royalist position towards Saltash, a dangerous manoeuvre, and Sir William Balfour was made responsible for this. Essex proposed to take the infantry to Fowey and to escape by sea. The Royalists, anticipating these moves, garrisoned a cottage on the Lostwithiel to Liskeard road with fifty fusiliers, and the armies in the hills were alerted and put on guard.

Under the cover of darkness and fog, on the night of 30/31 August, 2,500 cavalry silently made their way through the Royalist army unmolested. The fusiliers in the cottage were asleep or drunk, and the army 'on guard' were straggled abroad foraging for provisions.

Only the Earl of Cleveland with 100 horsemen faced the enemy on the hill but, with so few men, he dared not attack. Later, when the King arrived with reinforcements, Cleveland attacked their rear, too late to make much impression. The rebels escaped to Plymouth.

There were bitter recriminations to follow, but now the King mustered what infantry he could and at 7 am marched into Lostwithiel with 1,000 men. The rebels were already retreating to Fowey, having mined the bridge to hinder the Royalist approach. Luckily this had been observed, and the mine was defused.

Even as they retreated, the rebels found time for vandalism. Two Royalist gentlemen imprisoned in the Church had climbed into the tower and were mocking the retreating soldiers. Angered, the rebels tried to smoke them out by burning damp hay, then fired muskets at them from inside the tower. As neither of these brought the men down, they ignited a barrel of gunpowder inside the Church, which damaged the roof, but the prisoners remained unharmed.

The Royalists chased the rebels from field to field, and there was bitter fighting all the way to Castle Dore, where Essex made a stand. His men were weary and disheartened and it came to nought. The King spent that night in the shelter of a hedge with his men. Meanwhile, Essex and several of his officers slipped quietly away and escaped, probably by boat, leaving General Skippon to surrender. The Royalists were generous; officers were allowed to keep their arms and the sick and wounded were cared for in Fowey. The 6,000 fit men were to march under escort to Poole; Symonds describes the exodus on Monday 2 September: 'it rained extremely as the Varlets marched away . . . pressed all of a heap like sheep, so dirty and dejected it was rare to see'.

The escorts, even with drawn swords, could not prevent the Royalist soldiers from mocking and robbing the prisoners, but this was as nothing compared with what awaited them in Lostwithiel. The angry townspeople, especially the women, after weeks of starvation and degradation at their hands, attacked them 'tooth and nail', mocked, abused and stripped them of their clothes and their boots, before driving them across the bridge, defeated and disgraced. Only 1,000 of the 6,000 men reached Poole. A few escaped to Plymouth, but most died of exhaustion or plague, or were set upon and murdered on the way. The King left the county on 5 September saying 'Dear Mr Sheriff, I leave Cornwall to you safe and sound'.

He left Lostwithiel, a town shattered and starving, and prey to a pestilence that killed many of its people. The surrounding land was trampled and broken, with nothing left to harvest. It took many years to recover. Gradually the markets and the industries revived, and the buildings were repaired. The Great Hall never did recover completely, although parts of it were repaired and used again.

The *Sealed Knot Society* re-enacts the battles of the Civil War from time to time. (CPB)

Over the next few decades a number of modest but substantial houses were built. Some were later converted into shops. These 17th century buildings can be seen all over the town, in Fore Street, North Street, Tanhouse Lane, in Queen Street, then called Ducken Street (there was probably a ducking stool over the mill pond, near the site of Mill Gardens) and on Bodmin Hill, then called Crockerne Street. In 1688 a piece of land on Terras Hill was leased to Melchisedek Woen, a husbandman of Lostwithiel, who probably built Mount Pleasant on the corner of Bodmin Hill. There is still a Jewish emblem on the eastern gable. At last the rebuilding was under way and Lostwithiel was recovering from its ordeal.

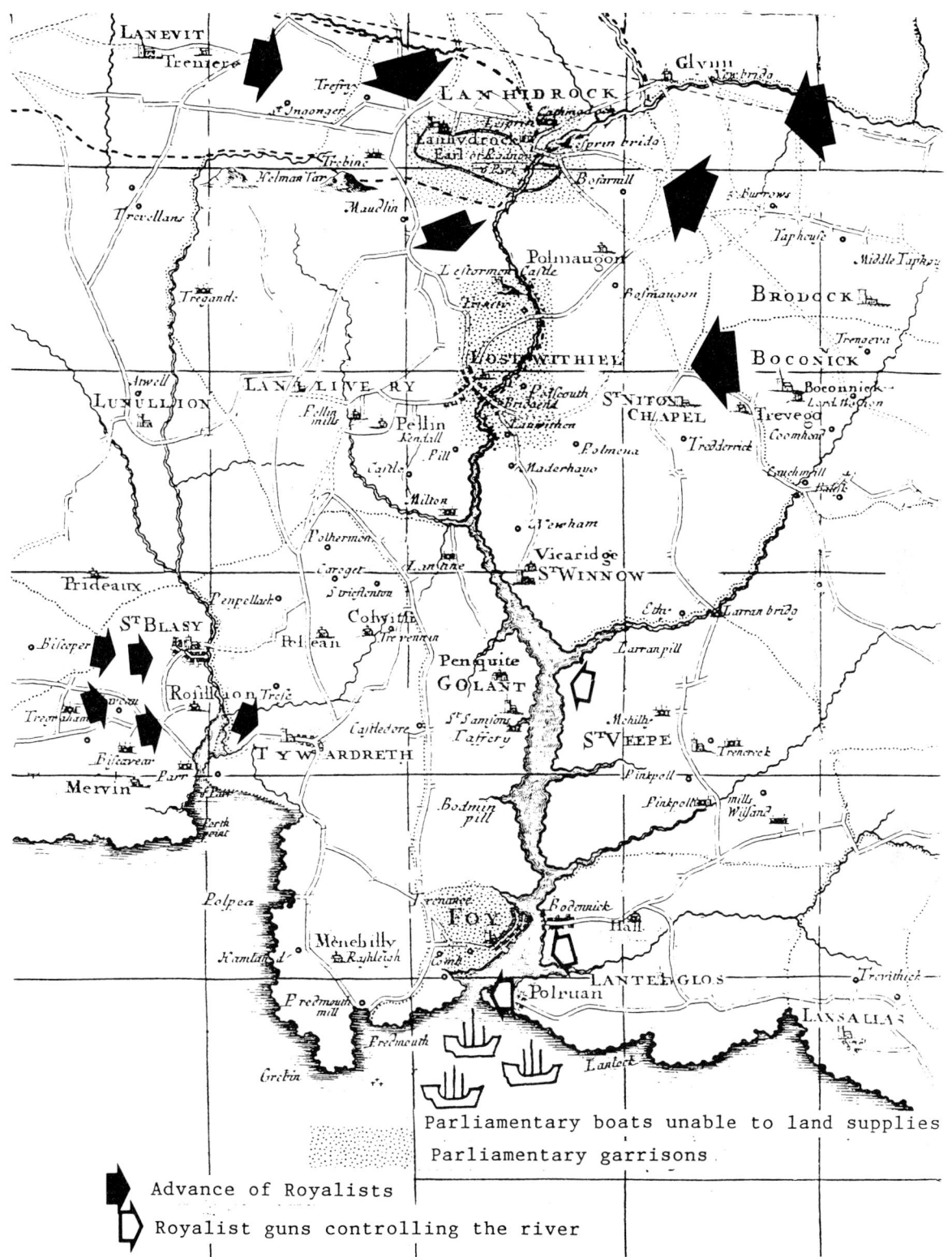

The Siege of Lostwithiel: Essex's army was surrounded and trapped by Royalists; based on Gascoyne's map, 1699. (DCRS) (IF)

LEFT: There was rebuilding after the Civil War. (IF) ABOVE: Lease stone on the Malt House — for 3,000 years. This was once part of Taprell House. (IF) RIGHT: Gable of Mount Pleasant, Bodmin Hill, late 17th century, showing the Star of David (Jewish emblem) and a window blocked to reduce tax, introduced towards the end of the century. (IF)

A Rat mad for the Dutys on houses with in the Borow of Lostwithiell for the year 1735

Name	£	s	Name	£	s
Thomas Elett maior x	2	0	a hous Thomas Lean Lives in x	2	0
Richard Egcomb Esq x	2	0	a hous Ann Philips Lives in x	2	0
Richard Couch x	2	0	a hous Francis Lenarvn Lives in x	2	0
John Arthur x	6	0	John styll x	2	0
William Samuell x	6	0	John westlak x	2	0
Samuell Philips x	6	0	a hous James Haly Lives in	2	0
Phily Duret x	6	0	Docter wadam x	2	0
nicholas Reed	2	0	Hugh Tremear x	2	0
nicholas Lee Chandler x	2	0	a hous Stephen may Lives in x	2	0
Jams Robins x	2	0	John Heans	2	0
Charity Lyly x	2	0	Nicholas strong	2	0
Embling Truebody x	2	0	Francis Jams	2	0
Wm Carnick x	2	0	John Spiller x	2	0
nicholas Lee quaker	2	0	John	2	0
Elizabeth Johns x	2	0	Piter Colmer x	2	0
nicholas Hoob x	2	0			
margret Johns x	2	0			
Ralph Crips x	2	0			
Frances wills Hous x	2	0			
Joseph Hurtridg x	2	0			
Stephen Tonking x	2	0			
the orphnt of Henry Jams x	2	0			
Thomas Band	2	0			
John Polard x	2	0			
Robert moor x	2	0			
John Haly	2	0			
mary millwart x	2	0			

Seen & allowed this 21th day of October 1735 by
Tho. Eliott mayor
Rich.d Couch Dep-Recorder

Page of duties charged on houses (Window Tax), 1735. (CRO)

LEFT: The oldest monument in the Church; the brass in memory of Tristram Curteys of Pill, 1423. (SBC) (IF) RIGHT: A drawing of the brass by FMH, 1891. (RIC) BELOW: Pelyn House, home of the Kendal family, partly rebuilt after the 19th century fire. (IF)

Power and Influence

Through the centuries, particularly before 1832, there were families who attained power and influence, mainly by means of their wealth. While some used the town to gain access to Parliament for their sons and allies, others were genuinely concerned for the wellbeing of the town and county. The Pitts produced Prime Ministers, the Kendals, Robartes and Edgecumbes were MPs. Other families, among them Taprells, Johns, Norways, Hexts and Fosters, had a more local influence as Recorders and Mayors.

Until 1832 Lostwithiel was represented in Parliament by two MPS. Lostwithiel's first MPs were Stephen le Rede and Randolph Curteys of Pill, in 1304. Over the next 100 years Curteyses represented the town in Parliament many more times. Tristram Curteys was MP in 1421, and the oldest monument in the Parish Church is a brass in his memory. His status was that of a landowner of free, but not noble birth, a 'franklin'. He would have been expected to supply infantry men in time of war. Seventy years later, his descendant Richard Curteys enclosed the Town Land.

The Kendals of Pelyn have the longest association with Lostwithiel, for they were here for over 600 years. John de Kendale, Receiver for the Black Prince in 1351, handed the office to his son in 1365. The Prince offered John a knighthood, which he refused, saying 'on my estate the farmers are my tenants and my friends. If I accept a knighthood I shall be above them and I wish to be with them'. Lands at Pelyn were granted to the Kendals, who lived there until Mr Nicholas Kendal died in March 1992, leaving the manor house to the charity Help the Aged. Kendals represented Lostwithiel in Parliament in 1365 and on at least 20 occasions over 400 years: William, MP in 1570, is remembered as a generous host; Nicholas, MP in 1640, died fighting for the King's cause.

The Market Place in Lostwithiel was part of the Town Lands. Towards the end of the 16th century the trust was not well managed and, on the marriage of Catherine Hellyar to Walter Kendal, this land was illegally leased to them. There were also other instances that some did 'unlawfully make profits for themselves from Corporation property' in which Walter, Richard and Thomas Kendal and Ralph Taprell were all involved. In 1603 the Mayor and Corporation filed a complaint in the Chancery Court against those . . . 'who did keep and withhold from the said town the market place . . . and other trust lands'. The case ended in favour of the town.

Sons of the Kendal family served the town as Mayors and Recorders and the county as Magistrates and High Sheriffs. The late Mrs Dorothy de Lancey Nicholls, a much respected local historian and naturalist, was born a Kendal. There are memorials to the family in both Lostwithiel and Lanlivery Churches.

Over the years Boconnoc has had a history of turbulent young squires. In the 13th century Sir Thomas de Kencia raided Bishop Bronscombe's deep park, and 150 years later Sir Hugh Courtney indulged in piracy.

Sir William Mohun moved to Boconnoc in the late 16th century. His grandson, John, was created 1st Lord Mohun of Okehampton and it was he who hosted King Charles I at

Boconnoc during the Civil War (when it is said the King arrived by coach — the first coach to attempt to travel over Cornwall's rough tracks). The 5th Lord died as a result of duelling, the title became extinct and the estate was sold in about 1720 to Thomas Pitt.

Thomas Pitt had worked in India, traded in diamonds and became Governor of Madras. In 1701 he bought a magnificent diamond for £20,500. After cutting, it was claimed to be the finest in the world. Pitt offered it to Queen Anne, who refused it; he sold it in 1717 to the Duke of Orleans for £135,000.

With part of this money Thomas Pitt bought Boconnoc. He died in 1726, his eldest son Robert surviving him by one year. Boconnoc passed to Robert's son, Thomas, who became a Steward of the Duchy, Deputy Warden of the Stannaries and a Capital Burgess of Lostwithiel.

At the time Thomas inherited Boconnoc, his younger brother William was 18 years of age; William was destined for greatness, to become Prime Minister and later Earl of Chatham, a respected and revered statesman.

The son of Thomas Pitt was created Baron Camelford. The Baron's son Thomas, born in 1775, was baptised at Boconnoc amid great rejoicing. This young man's life illustrates the abuse of privilege. He grew up arrogant and without self-control but, no doubt owing to his highly placed kinsmen, he was pardoned for almost every misdemeanour. It seems that only George Vancouver disciplined him, and that to his cost. At the age of 16 Thomas Pitt joined Vancouver's ship *Discovery* on a five year voyage to survey and chart the west coast of North America.

Midshipman Pitt was, from the first, insubordinate and contemptuous of discipline, and brought on himself two well deserved floggings. In 1794 he flagrantly disobeyed orders and was put in irons for 10 days until he could be sent home. Two years later Vancouver returned to London. Lord Camelford (as he now was) had just come of age and had taken his seat in the House of Lords. He was lusting for revenge, and challenged Vancouver to a duel. Vancouver refused, for his treatment of an insubordinate midshpman had been exemplary and any complaint was a matter for a court martial. Camelford then assaulted Vancouver in the street. He managed to turn this to his advantage by buying biased newspaper reporting and a cartoon by Gillray *The Caneing in Conduit Street*. This circulated in London and throughout the ports, bringing undeserved ridicule upon Vancouver and leaving him heartbroken and without redress.

Vancouver died aged 41, in poverty: no state official attended his funeral, for he had dared to put a Pitt in irons. Meanwhile Camelford's bizarre behaviour continued; he attacked all who crossed him and killed more than once in illegal duels. His final duel was with a friend in 1804 when Thomas, 2nd Lord Camelford, was fatally wounded and died three days later, aged 29. The title became extinct and Boconnoc was inherited by his sister, Lady Grenville. In 1864 she gave the estate to her husband's nephew, the Hon George Fortescue and it remains with the Fortescue family today.

In the 16th century the Robartes of Lanhydrock were a Truro family trading mainly in wood and charcoal, the latter indispensable to tinners. They bought woodlands in all parts of the county and, after trees were felled, turned the land to agriculture. As they became richer they lent their money to tinners who paid their debts in tin.

Richard Roberts (later Robartes) bought the Lanhydrock estate and built his mansion. He was knighted in 1616 and in 1625, on payment of £12,000, was created Baron, at the Court of King James 1. The King, to ease his own financial situation, was persuading the newly rich to buy titles. The family built up a superb library, continued to buy land and married into older titled families, establishing their position as landed gentry.

It was Richard's son John who persuaded Lord Essex to bring his Parliamentary army to Cornwall in 1644. He was nevertheless appointed Recorder of Lostwithiel in 1647. By 1660 he was a Royalist, accepted by Charles II and later created Earl Radnor.

The Robartes lived at Lanhydrock for over 300 years, inheriting the title Viscount Clifden. The 6th Lord Clifden gave the house to the National Trust in 1953; he continued to live there until his death in 1966. His son, the 7th Lord Clifden, moved away and died without a male heir in 1974. Older residents of Lostwithiel remember the Robartes with affection. The beautiful gardens at Lanhydrock are being developed continually and are a constant source of delight.

Between 1705-1733 a family called John monopolised the Mayoralty of Lostwithiel. W. P. Courtney in his *Parliamentary Representation of Cornwall in 1832* (1889) says 'The Mayoralty of Lostwithiel might be called the perquisite of the family John for, by means of bribes and threats etc. it remained with one or other of them during at least 20 years. The satellites of the then Prince of Wales knew the value of the family and plied them with blandishments of the most persuasive kind, in the hope of obtaining a footing in the constituency'.

In 1705 Russell Robartes and Sir John Molesworth, both Tories, were elected to Parliament. James Kendal petitioned against this return, establishing his right to the place taken by Molesworth. The Mayor, John John, had arbitrarily disenfranchised several Burgesses before the election.

Again there was malpractice in 1708 by Alexander John, Mayor and Returning Officer. Votes cast in the election were Hon Francis Robartes (Tory) 20, Hon Russell Robartes (Tory) 17, Mr James Kendal (Whig) 5, Mr Joseph Additon (Whig) 4, and Mr Kendal and Mr Addison were declated duly elected. It took three petitions and 19 months before the Robartes were declared the rightful MPs for Lostwithiel. Joseph Addison was the well known essayist described as 'one of the most illustrious ornaments of his time'.

The Taprells came to Lostwithiel early in the 17th century from the St Neot area. Ralph died in 1621. In 1640 John Taprell, chandler, leased a mansion on the south side of Fore Street, probably on the site of the present Guildhall. His brother, William, who is thought to have lived in the house known as Taprell House, was Mayor in 1644 during the miserable days of the siege. A William Taprell, innkeeper, lived here in 1672, his inn perhaps on the site of the adjoining King's Arms. Members of the family held the Mayoralty of the town on several occasions until the end of the century, after which they appear to have moved away. The last local records relating to the family are of the death of a John Taprell in 1725 and a Miss Martha in 1735.

The Edgcumbes, a rich and influential family of east Cornwall, first came to Lostwithiel and bought property towards the end of the Johns' hold on the Mayoralty. Richard Edgcumbe was made Recorder for the town in 1733; the following year he was the MP and in 1738, the Mayor. According to the W. P. Courtney, Mr Edgcumbe was 'The main manager of the little Cornish Boroughs in the interest of Sir Robert Walpole. So great was Mr Edgcumbe's knowledge of the secrets of these constituencies that he was created a peer . . . in order that the privileges of the Upper House might shield him from examination by the Select Committee, should one have been appointed'.

For 100 years the Edgcumbes controlled Lostwithiel. The position of Recorder was handed down from father to son.

The family bought Taprell House for their own use, and modernised it in the fashion of the day, giving it an imposing granite frontage onto Fore Street, later doing the same for the part of the building now known as the Dower House. They developed the building across the road into the Guildhall, Corn Market and Town Gaol, and built the Market Hall and Grammar School and the New Talbot Hotel (which was on North Street). They bought up other properties in the town and took over the living of the Church.

W. P. Courtney, in a footnote writes that a 'distinguished native of Lostwithiel' (in 1890) informed him that traditionally the Pitts of Boconnoc controlled the Borough, giving £6 to each of the 17 Councillors at election time. The seven Aldermen received no money, but official posts were secured for them. At the election following the advent of the Edgcumbes, surprisingly, the Pitt candidates were not elected. It seems the Councillors had been paid £30 each for their votes, and Aldermen had been offered Edgcumbe property at low rents. So it continued until 1832. The Edgcumbes however achieved no promotion in Parliament, once the Pitts took office, but the 214 electors continued to return their patron's nominee.

Lostwithiel was no better or worse than most other 'pocket boroughs', and the Reform Act of 1832 was well overdue when it swept them all away, and Lostwithiel became part of a larger, more democratic constituency.

The Edgcumbes, having no reason now to stay in Lostwithiel, withdrew, and over a period of 80 years sold off their considerable property in the town.

The Fosters were tanners in Lostwithiel who grew rich in the 18th century and bought Castle, the country house near Lantyan. The valley was cold and sunless, as its Cornish name implies, and in 1829 they bought land and built Lanwithan, which enjoys the sun all day. They became bankers, building Fosters Bank (now Barclays) and marrying into other banking families. In the second half of the 19th century they served the town as Mayors and helped to finance the building of the Bodmin Hill and St Winnow Schools. They built St Saviour's Chapel and the Reading Room at Bridgend. Although, in the 19th century 13 children wre born to the family, no male Fosters survive today, and the present owner of Lanwithan, Mr Richard Foster Edward-Collins, inherited through the female line.

George Bell Lawrance, born in 1776, bought No 11 Bodmin Hill and married Miss Dorothea Bullock Bennett of Lostwithiel in 1814. George had already had an exciting career in the Royal Navy, seeing much action around the world. He served as Master's Mate with Captain William Bligh on the *Director* in 1799-1800, and as Lieutenant to Rear Admiral Sir Samuel Hood aboard *Centaur* from 1806-1810. He last saw active service in 1811.

Some time later he occupied No 32 Fore Street and ran a Naval training establishment there. There are still rings in the bedroom walls where the boys' hammocks were slung, and an outside stairway leading from the dormitories to the yard and boat house. George Lawrance retired from the Royal Navy in 1840 with the rank of Commander and sold his Bodmin Hill property in 1843. He was also an artist, and has left delightful drawings and watercolours of Lostwithiel. He died in 1846. Memorials to Commander Lawrance and his family are near the north porch in the Church.

The Globe Inn was the private house of the Norways from the late 17th century. When Captain Norway retired from the East India Company in 1753, he started to build Norway House. It passed to his nephew, Neville, newly married to Sarah Arthur of the Crown & Sceptre. Norway House is solidly built and has exceptionally fine cellars, it faces the river but is well hidden behind tall trees; the drive sweeps round and runs diagonally down the quay. Neville Norway set up as a merchant banker, and also took over both the Crown & Sceptre and the Kings Arms. One can only wonder what his uncle's plans for the house were, and if there was a connection between the ease of access from the quay to the cellars and the ownership of two taverns. Neville was Mayor of the town in his old age. Arthur H. Norway, writer of *Highways and Byways of Devon and Cornwall* was of this family, as was Neville Shute, the Australian novelist. The house is now divided into three spacious dwellings.

The Hexts were a professional family of lawyers and army officers, who came to Lostwithiel from Trenarren in the mid-18th century. They had a town house, 23 North Street, and for a while leased Restormel House. They built Cowbridge on the hillside. The Hexts were Mayors on 18 occasions, over a period of 135 years. Miss Frances Hext is remembered for her book *Memorials of Lostwithiel* which she published privately in 1891.

In 1915 a young army Captain, Robert Howe was billeted at Cowbridge. He and Miss Loveday Hext, who is still remembered as very beautiful, fell in love. The Hexts disapproved, for Robert, although he had graduated well from Cambridge, was of a lower social class. However, the two were married, Robert went on to earn a knighthood and became the Governor General of the Sudan. They retired to Cowbridge and were involved with the life of the town. Sir Robert served as Mayor by invitation in 1958. Since his death in 1981, Cowbridge has been sold and has become a Nursing Home.

All these families have left their mark one way or another, not least by their houses, which still grace our town and countryside.

The influence of John Wesley on the town was of a different order. John Wesley first came to Cornwall in 1743, and found among the Cornish people a predisposition to receive his message. He came regularly to the county, making 32 visits over 46 years. His only visit to Lostwithiel was just two years before his death, when he was 86 years old. He noted in his journal '11 am Monday August 17th (1789) Lostwithiel talk'.

1790 saw the opening of a Wesleyan Chapel in King Street. Methodism, as it came to be called, attracted people of all social classes. It became a separate, free Church, and later there were a number of secessions from the main Wesleyan movement. Each branch of Methodism had its adherents. Although making a late start in Lostwithiel, Methodism became strong in the town. In 1837 a Methodist United Free Church was opened on the Bank, and in 1859 a Primitive Methodist Chapel was built in Bridgend. Before 1880 a Congregational Chapel had been built on Restormel Road. Many craftsmen and tradespeople in the town joined these nonconformist movements and were known as 'dissenters'.

As soon as there was a free election for local Councillors (1885), dissenters began to take an active part in local government. There had been discrimination against nonconformists for over a century. Not until 1828 were they allowed to hold office in national or local government. All baptisms and marriages had to be registered at the Parish Church until 1838, and it was not until 1880 that conformist ministers were allowed to officiate at burials in consecrated ground.

As the Chapel congregations grew in numbers and wealth, they replaced their early chapels with bigger and better buildingts. In 1880 the Wesleyans built a large Victorian Gothic Church (where the Royal Talbot Hotel car park now is) moving out of their origianl Chapel, which was converted into houses. In 1900 the United Free Methodists built a large granite fronted Chapel on the Bank.

The town would appear to have been fairly evenly divided between Church and Chapel, and for many years regular Sunday worship was part of the family life for most people. But Church and Chapel-going was to decline, and the Congregational Church was closed before the 1920s and converted into houses.

When the Methodist Church was reunited in 1932 it became clear that all these chapels were not needed. The Primitive Methodist Chapel was first to close in 1933, and became a dwelling. In the 1960s there was a dilemma as to which of the two big Chapels, standing almost side by side, should be kept and which should go. It was a time of great unhappiness for those concerned. Eventually, although agreement had been reached to keep open the Wesleyan Chapel, the decision was reversed, and this was the one to be closed, and later demolished.

The number of worshippers continued to decline and only 20 years later in 1987, the Bank Chapel, now too big and expensive for the small congregation to maintain, was also closed and sold to be converted into flats. After this the Methodist community used St Saviour's Chapel as their place of worship, until the opening on 29 February 1993 of a Chapel and meeting rooms within the refurbished Taprell House.

FAR LEFT: Florence Netherton at the front door of Pelyn with Sally, the Kendals' dog — 1930s. (B&FM) CENTRE: Thomas Pitt with the diamond in his hat, painted by Sir Godfrey Kneller. With part of the profits from its sale he bought Boconnoc. (This picture is on loan to Plymouth Museum and Art Gallery) (JGDF) LEFT: Boconnoc House; the Estate still has a deer park. BELOW: Restormel House on the site of the Chapel of the Holy Trinity. (DB) ABOVE: *The Caneing in Conduit Street* — cartoon of Lord Camelford's assault upon George Vancouver, by James Gillray, 1796. (BM)

LEFT: Richard, 1st Lord Robartes, painted by Cornelius Jonson. (NT)
RIGHT: 1st Lord Edgcumbe; portrait in Lostwithiel Guildhall, attributed to Reynolds. (LTC) (JB) BELOW: The Guildhall and Corn Market, built 1740, photographed in 1890. (FMH) (LSC)

ABOVE: Lanhydrock House before the fire of 1881. (LM) BELOW: The Market Hall and Grammar School above, built 1781, photographed in 1890. (FMH) (LSC)

ABOVE: Fore Street 1825; watercolour by George Bell Lawrance, showing his house on the right, now Centra Stores. (RFE-C) INSET: Lawrances family crest incorporated that of his wife, née Bennett; it was in his house at 23, Fore Street. (LM) BELOW: The carriage awaits . . . at the front door of Lanwithan House, 1880. (RFE-C)

ABOVE: A wedding in the Foster family — 1880s. (RFE-C) LEFT: Norway House, built beside the quay and hidden by trees. (V&AM) RIGHT: Miss Frances M. Hext, author of *Memorials of Lostwithiel and Restormel*, 1891. (LM)

LEFT: Captain Robert Howe on right, with A Co, 13 Battalion, Sherwood Foresters in Monmouth Square; a recruiting march in 1915. (LM). RIGHT: The Congregational Chapel, built before 1880, was converted to houses (Glentworth Terrace) before 1920. (LTC) BELOW: View from Terras Hill 1880 showing 1st Wesleyan Chapel on right (King Street). (RFE-C)

ABOVE: The 2nd Wesleyan Chapel, demolished in the 1960s. (CPB)
BELOW: Laying foundation stones for the new Bank Chapel, 1900,
John Santo in top hat. (LM)

ABOVE: The Bank Chapel 1900-1987, now converted to flats. (LM)
BELOW: The new Methodist Chapel, opened 20 February 1993. (JB)

Into the 19th Century

Few coaches ventured into Cornwall before the Turnpike Act of 1751, whereby users paid a toll towards the upkeep of roads. Until then travellers rode on horseback or walked over the rough tracks. Goods were carried by packhorse or sea and river.

The first stage-coach between Torpoint and Truro called at Lostwithiel in 1796. After this Lostwithiel was soon established as a staging post. In November 1806 the first *Royal Mail* coach from Plymouth to Falmouth *via* Lostwithiel, was ferried over the Tamar, loaded with letters. (William Manley Birch started his Plymouth stage service in 1796 — his great-great grandson is the publisher of this book.) Soon towns along the route were relying on the coaches for news from London, which they had never previously received so regularly. This was especially important during the Napoleonic war with France.

The *Royal Cornwall Gazette* reported Lostwithiel's reaction to news of peace on 16 April 1814. 'The populace ... went forth in crowds ... to meet the mail, and draw it by hand into the town ... Every individual in the place wore a white cockade and all the houses were decked with laurel and many with flags'. Unfortunately in the excitement, two men were run over by the coach and badly injured.

In 1832 the 'reformers' were waiting up to meet the coach bringing news of the passing of the Reform Act. It reached Lostwithiel at 4 am whereupon 'a band of music made the valley resound'. The improvement in the roads increased opportunities for trade, and the inns and taverns did good business.

From the early 19th century, coastal vessels carried limestone as ballast from Plymouth to Fowey, barged upriver to Lostwithiel kilns to be converted to lime for agricultural use. Iron ore, leather, meat and fish were sent downriver to be shipped from Fowey.

In the mid-19th century proposals were made by Richard Foster Esq for the construction of a ship canal between Golant and Lostwithiel, to allow passage of vessels up to 200 tons. Estimates showed that the canal would be uneconomic, particularly as there would soon be a railway, and the project was abandoned.

Towards the end of the 18th century the difference between rich and poor became much more marked. The price of bread increased threefold between 1792-1812, and there were a few destitute people in the town who, under the Poor Law, were the responsibility of the Parish. A Vestry Book recorded the Parish's care for the poor between 1781-1825.

Parishioners paid a 'poor rate' and overseers were appointed to manage the money. The first entry in the book records that on 17 April 1781 there were seven women and six children receiving between 1s and 2s a week each. The Vestry Book indicates the nature of discussion: '6th May 1787 Margaret Trevleavan shall be allowed in future 2/- a week ... she appearing to us to be an object worthy of such pay'. Parishes accepted responsibility for those born in them: '16th May 1784, We ... agree unanimously that Grace Roberts and Alice Roberts, two paupers of this parish, now lodged in Padstow Workhouse (for divers reasons) shall be fetched home ...'

By 1790 there was a poor house: '... that 2/6 a week be allowed to Thomas Williams, a pauper, now in the poor house'. Clothes and tools were issued; '3rd February 1793, Peter Trevleaven be supplied with a coat, waistcoat, breeches, stockings and shirt'. In 1820 John

Vane received a new spade. Nancy Leavers was not so lucky. She applied for an oven, flour and fuel to start up a 'penny pie business'. But, as many ratepayers were in that same line, it was judged that 'an injury could be done to them by granting it'. In 1798 Richard Foster, a wealthy tanner, negotiated to buy the Poor House, which was near his home, and to provide another, some distance away. It seems the 'boghouse' was a public nuisance.

The children of paupers were put out to 'apprenticeships'. To make this more attractive to prospective masters, a sum of money went with them. In May 1800 it was agreed to give a tradesman £4 with a boy and £6 with a girl, while others of lower status taking 'apprentices' were to receive £2 'to clothe the child'.

The distribution of the poor rate applied only to Lostwithiel Parish. People living south of the River Cober, in Summer Lane, Tangier (Castle Hill) and the Moors, were in Lanlivery Parish and not entitled to help from St Bartholomew's. This was the poorest part of the Borough, and received little, if any, help from its own parish.

By 1800 the Stannary gaol was being used for debtors. It was described in 1805 by an official, James Nield, as being 'very dirty, not having been white-washed for nearly thirty years'. One of the last debtors to be imprisoned here was a St Agnes man, Salathiel Harris. No food was provided so, to save the poor man from starvation during four months in prison, the gaoler brought him down to an iron grated window by the street 'there to solicit the casual charity of passers-by, by means of a shoe suspended by a cord with which the keeper had humanely provided him'.

No sooner was Lostwithiel celebrating peace in Europe, than soldiers were marching through the town to Plymouth to embark for America. The *West Briton* of 26 August 1814 reported a local tragedy. After the military baggage had gone through the town, four drunken men remained behind, two of whom were incapable of walking. One soldier asked the constable for a cart to convey these two to the next town, but the constable refused. The soldiers loaded their muskets and threatened to shoot. One soldier fired, but the powder only flashed in the pan. The Town Sergeant, Joseph Burnett, arrived saying he would 'take into custody him who fired'. The soldier replied 'I'll shoot you first' and fired twice. The second ball passed through Burnett's body, striking another man, Walter Davies, and both fell. Spectators secured the soldiers. Burnett died within half an hour, leaving nine children; Davies died three days later, leaving five children. John Sims and Richard Rogers were committed on a charge of wilful murder. Richard Rogers was acquitted, but John Sims was found guilty and hanged on 31 March 1915 at Launceston. It was reported in *The Star* that 'his behaviour at the place of execution was marked by contrition and manly fortitude'.

1812 was a year when corn was scarce, prices were high and there was much hardship. A local scheme was introduced to subsidise the sale of barley. Thomas Hext made an interest-free loan to the overseers to buy barley, for resale at a cheaper rate. Seventy families, about a quarter of the population, benefitted. When all the corn was sold there was a deficit of just £27, borne by the poor rate. There was satisfaction the scheme had worked so well.

After the Napoleonic Wars, the level of unemployment was such that the Lostwithiel Vestry could barely cope. A scheme was set up between 1819-22 and again between 1825-29 whereby unemployed men worked in the town quarry on Terras Hill. They received low wages, but this was seen as preferable to idleness on Parish support. The venture lost money; tools had to be provided, the men were initially unskilled, and there were few markets for the stone during the depression. In six years £97 had been spent and income had been £52 6s 1½d. The money spent was offset by the non-payment of 'relief'; the men had been occupied and paid for their labour, and the overseers were content with this scheme also.

In 1812, perhaps driven by hardship, the men of St Neot came one night to Lostwithiel, and destroyed the salmon weir, which lay above the bridge. They believed this weir prevented the fish from reaching their part of the river. In 1990 during construction of the golf course, broken granite blocks and mangled iron bars were found — the remains of a night's destruction nearly 200 years ago.

In contrast to the poverty was the leisured life of the rich. Mr & Mrs Thomas Staniforth of Liverpool spent four months in 1800 with their daughter Mrs Hext at Restormel House. In his diary Thomas Staniforth wrote 'Saturday 16th August. Morning very bright, hot sun. At 10 Hext and I set out on horseback for Boconnoc, the seat of Lord Camelford ... Wednesday 20th August. Entered my journal and amused myself in reading. Mr Tho Hext came and dined and drank tea with us'.

On 27 August there began a sequence of entries illustrating the great advance in medical science which perhaps we now take for granted. John Hext's father Samuel 'was in a very alarming state in consequence of a suppression of urine. Dr Hall of Bodmin came over at 8 ... Samuel passed a most painful day without any evacuation, not having had resolution to undergo the operation of a catheter, though he attempted it more than once, which distressed us all very much for fear of an inflammation, which might deprive us of so good and valuable a man in the course of a few hours. Dr Hall sleeps there'.

During the week Samuel's condition deteriorated. He was unable to resort to a catheter and the doctors could do nothing to save him, although attending him constantly. He died after eight days of suffering, and the funeral took place at midnight of September 8/9 'according to the custom of the country when any person of consequence is buried'.

Between the extremes of rich and poor came the majority of Lostwithiel's solid citizens, who paid the poor rate and from among whom came the churchwardens, overseers and assistant councillors.

The Grammar School was founded by the Corporation in about 1770 and was probably house originally in the Guildhall. There were no endowments, but the Corporation paid £20 a year towards costs, and nominated six boys for free education.

In 1781 the Market Hall was built, the upstairs area intended for an Assembly Room; this however became the Grammar School. A succession of masters taught in the school, most of them clergymen, for an annual salary of about £50. A writing master was also employed, for £20 a years. The school closed in 1842. A Commercial School, using the Guildhall as a base, moved into the Grammar School premises and continued into the 1880s.

The development of the Restormel Iron Mines brought work at last to Lostwithiel. The mines flourished and were at their zenith in the 1830s. In 1836 tramlines were laid to Lostwithiel wharf, speeding the transport of ore. From here it was barged to Fowey.

The success of the iron mines gave a great boost to the economy. People were attracted to the town, not only to work in the mines, but to trade and to pursue their crafts. In the ten years between 1831-41 the population (including Bridgend) is estimated to have increased from 1,110 to 1,850, (66%). Speculative builders were at work putting up rows of cheaply built 'workers' cottages'. These had two rooms upstairs, and one downstairs, only one exterior door, tiny windows, no plumbing and no gardens. They were called after their builders: Eveleighs' Row, Knights Row, Philp's Court and others. They were insanitary and overcrowded and soon degenerated. Many were pulled down before the end of the century, and most have now been demolished.

Several substantial houses of the period, built or restyled for the more wealthy residents, were later converted into shops. The architectural refinements beyond and above the shops are seldom suspected by the casual shopper. Those which are still dwellings retain their early 19th century dignity.

During the first decades of the century Lostwithiel lost some of its county importance. In 1832 the County Courts were moved to Bodmin, and after that year there were no more elections of 'Knights of the Shire' to Parliament, attracting crowds from all over the county to Lostwithiel to cast their votes. However, the town was busy and growing, and welcomed the Victorian era in good heart.

LEFT: Early 19th century milestone at Parish boundary. (IF) RIGHT: The flood of 1839, North Street; contemporary watercolour. (RFE-C)
BELOW: Receipt for work done on the Poor House by Wm Matthews, 1785. (CRO)

ABOVE: Early photograph of Duchy buildings, Stannary prison on left. The tramlines ran from iron mines to wharf. (DB) BELOW: Contemporary painting shows tramlines and horse-drawn wagons between mines and wharf at Lostwithiel, 1840s. (RFE-C)

LEFT: Tin miner, early 19th century, painted by Lawrance. (RFE-C)
RIGHT: Lostwithiel from the Liskeard Road, drawn by Lawrance. (RFE-C) BELOW: Town stocks, now in the south porch of the Church. (SBC) (IF) OPPOSITE: Poster of 1822. (CRO)

BOROUGH OF LOSTWITHIEL.

BY

A BY - LAW,

MADE BY THE

Mayor, Aldermen, and Assistants, of the said Borough,

The 24th Day of October, 1822,

IT IS PROVIDED,

THAT IF ANY

WAGGON, CART, CARRIAGE, or HORSE,

Shall be left standing and remaining within the Streets or Roads of the said Borough, unattended by any Driver, or other Person under whose care the same ought to be, the Owner shall forfeit and pay for every such Cart, Carriage, or Horse, any sum not exceeding

TEN SHILLINGS,

AS THE MAYOR SHALL ADJUDGE.

That no Person may plead Ignorance of this Law, it has been thought adviseable to make it thus Public, as the Mayor strictly intends to enforce it.

By order of the Mayor,

BENNETT, Town - Clerk.

Dated Lostwithiel, October 24, 1822.

Liddell and Son, Printers, Bodmin.

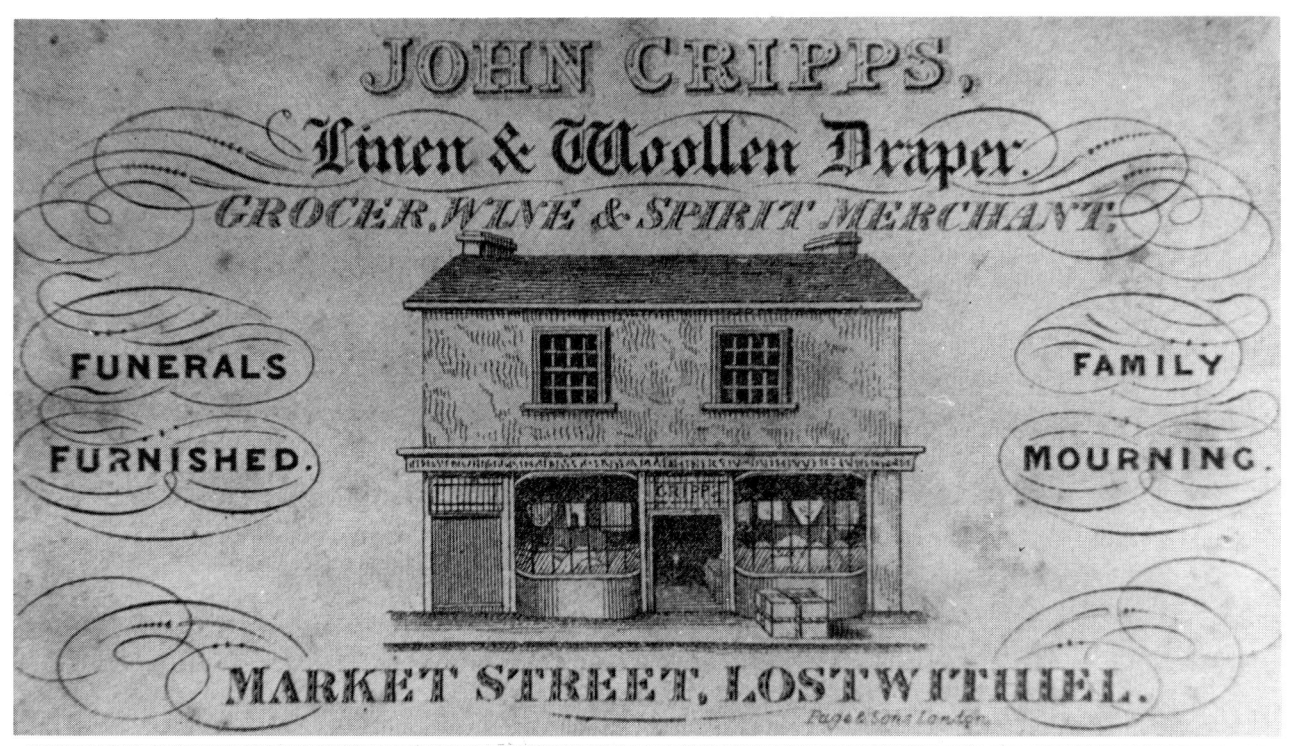

ABOVE: Market Street was called Queen Street after HM Queen Victoria's visit in 1846. (LM) BELOW: Lostwithiel Bridge painted by Lawrance (RFE-C)

The Victorian Era

It was a proud day for Lostwithiel when Queen Victoria, aged 27, came with her consort, Prince Albert, to visit the Restormel Iron Mine (below the Castle). It was the first visit of a sovereign since Charles I had routed the Parliamentary Army here in 1644. This was 8 September 1846 and the Queen wrote in her diary, 'We drove [from Fowey] through some of the narrowest streets I ever saw in England'. She described Restormel Castle as 'very picturesque' and goes on, 'We visited here Restormel Mine. It is an iron mine. Albert and I got into one of the trucks and were dragged in by miners. The miners wore a curious woollen dress with a cap . . . There was something unearthly about this lit up cavern place . . . The miners seemd so pleased at seeing us and are intelligent good people . . . It was quite dazzling when we came into daylight again'.

On 25 September the *Royal Cornwall Gazette* printed a copy of a miner's official report of the visit — 'D Sir this is to let you know that I have Higher Honour of Conducting the Queen Victoria and Prince Albert Und grownd yesterday the 8th of Sept. I can assure you I Laboured hard to Make evey Nesary Preparation for her Majesty and the Prince to go und grownd and so Did Cook. We first Warranted perfectly safety we prepared 5 ungrownd Wagons and the queen and Prince Albert went in the first Wagon. Mr. t. . walked in through the level and I by his Side Conducting queen and Prince Albert with 4 pulling Wagon By a Roope. . . . Upwards of 200 fathoms then the queen and Prince walked 14 fathoms through the level. I put the Pick in Prince Albert's hands Wich he took it And broke a stone of ore. I Hold My Hat for him to break it in. He took it out of the Hat and Put It in his pocket. I am happy to let you know That we never Make the least Shade of Blunder Whatever I have I ham thankful I know Not how to express myself to you for your kindness had it not been for you I should never had had the high Honour conducting her Majesty undgrownd, our Mine is working favourably. Wee are well thank God for it'.

In 1860 an enquiry was held into the cause of the decrease in the salmon fisheries. The iron mines were polluting the river with poisons. Apprentices and servants, who ate salmon at least twice a week, had in earlier days petitioned their masters for a change of diet, blaming the salmon for making them feel ill. We now know that fish in polluted waters, while tolerating the poisons in their own systems, can be poisonous to anyone eating them.

There were various other mining ventures around Lostwithiel, notably the silver lead mine at Boconnoc Silver Vein. This last never lived up to expectations.

Norman Pound's analyses of census returns for 1841 and 1851 show that, although the population was growing overall, young men between ten years and 35 years of age were leaving Lostwithiel. Ten years was considered a suitable age to start looking for work. There was plenty of work for women and girls; fifty-seven were employed as domestic servants, living in their masters' houses.

The 1841 census gives the occupation of 475 persons, mostly heads of households. Thirty-eight were of independent means, 187 were craftsmen, 93 were in agriculture, 51 were merchants, including retailers and hawkers, 54 were miners. There were 27 professional men, including doctors, teachers, lawyers, agents and clerks, 14 bargemen, and nine unskilled workers. There was pressure on accommodation, and people with room to spare would take in lodgers; 54 were registered in 1851, ten lodged in one house in Fore Street, nine of whom were hawkers, a common occupation at that time.

Lostwithiel is well supplied with inns and taverns but years ago, when it was smaller, there were many more. Ann's Gallery was the Town Arms, at Bridgend was the Dolphin, opposite the Post Office was the Golden Eagle, Byways on Bodmin Hill was a 'kiddly' (having a six day licence to serve beer and cider). This was well placed for the miners to quench their thirsts, as they came down from the mines at the top of the hill. Where were the Sailors Arms, the Malt Shovel, the Crown & Sceptre and the London Inn?

Lostwithiel people always welcomed an opportunity to celebrate. In July 1846 there were music and dancing in the streets at the news of the passing of the Cornwall Railway Bill. It was almost 13 years before there was a railway. Negotiations to buy land took a long time but, when construction started, it brought employment. On 12 November 1858 the *Royal Cornwall Gazette* reported of Lostwithiel 'A great number of men are employed on the Cornwall Railway . . . and now the gas works employ many more men; so that lodgings for mechanics etc, are very badly to be obtained and this once dull town is now almost as busy as a beehive'.

In 1858 the foundation stone for the gas works was laid. It was sited on the Moors, conveniently placed for supplies of coal barged up river. In 1859 the gas works went into operation, and the main-line railway from Plymouth to Truro was opened. Lostwithiel not only had a station, but a large maintenance workshop was built here too. One can imagine the excitement of that year, the change in people's lives, with this sudden burst into modernity. The opening of the Lostwithiel-Fowey line ten years later added further to the town's economy, although it damaged the river traffic, as the main line had damaged the stage-coaching business.

The railway was a welcome and regular source of employment for many years, developing and extending well into the 20th century. Now, some main line trains stop at Lostwithiel, but for most fast 125 services, passengers have to go to Bodmin Parkway.

The early days of the railway were not without incident. At 10 pm one night in 1861, a truck containing four tons of hay caught fire in the tunnel near Lostwithiel. The fire lit up the countryside for miles around. The wooden station buildings were in danger, but the Company engineer managed to detach the truck and pass it under the water tank. In October 1874, one morning a loaded truck became detached at Doublebois Station and 'rushed down the line at Rapid Speed . . . until it reached Lostwithiel, a distance of nearly 10 miles. The line was fortunately clear of traffic . . .' *West Briton*.

In the mid-19th century there were intermittent outbreaks of cholera, and in 1833 the Stannary Prison was used as an isolation hospital. Consideration was given in 1862 to the laying of 'a common sewer from end to end through one of the streets'. The estimated cost was about £100. It is recorded that 'upon receiving this report, the Vestry passed a resolution to the effect that the construction of the drain was feasible but not expedient'.

The Mayor and Burgesses were held to be the Authority responsible for nuisance removal, but nothing was done. The monthly cattle markets held in Queen Street added greatly to the 'nuisance'. It was suggested that the market be moved to the Moors, to which came the sharp response in a letter to the *West Briton*, 1886 'clean streets done without trade or traffic will not provide [for] doctors' and butchers' bills'. At some later time, pipes were laid to carry untreated sewage into the river. On animal slaughtering days the river ran red.

Towards the end of the 19th century levels were driven into the hills in search of fresh water, which was then piped to convenient places. There were a number of 'shoots' in the town that many people can remember. The 'shoot' in Victoria is still used by many local people in preference to the tap water supplied now by the South West Water Company.

After 1870, when education became compulsory, the Elementary School and Master's House were built on Bodmin Hill. The land was given by Lord Edgcumbe, and the Corporation gave £355 19s 2d towards building costs. It was originally a Church of England foundation, but in 1886 it was made over to a non-demoninational School Board. Parents were expected to pay 2d a week for each child's education. In the early days many left school well before they were 12 years old, but most people grew up able to read and write.

St Faith's Diocesan Convent, founded in 1864, was run by Sisters of Mercy from a community in Wantage, Oxfordshire as a training home for 'wayward' girls (called then a penitentiary). The girls were trained in domestic work, particularly as laundresses, and the convent functioned as a laundry for a wide area. On leaving, most girls went into domestic service. The convent closed in 1950; its memorial plates are in St Nectan's Chapel. The building was later used as a Youth Hostel and is now a private dwelling.

In 1874 the Shire Hall buildings were sold off in lots to tradesmen in the town. Four years later the Freemasons bought the Old Exchequer Hall and, having made repairs and alterations to meet their needs, they formally occupied it as a Masonic Hall in 1879.

In January 1876 a violent storm damaged the Church spire, not for the first time. When the spire had been repaired in 1757 it had not been raised to its original height, and had a stunted appearance. It was now decided to extend it by five feet, restoring its original elegance.

Other repairs to the Church were necessary; damp and wood decay were evident. Two years later the restoration of the Church was started. This was a fashionable Victorian phenomenon which has much to answer for. St Bartholomew's Church was closed for a year and services were held in the School on Bodmin Hill, which still belonged to the Church. Miss Hext in *Memorials of Lostwithiel* tells succinctly what happened. 'The whole interior was laid open, the old pews were cleared away, the gallery at the West end was taken down, the flooring was swept away and brought down level to the bases of the pillars . . . the vaults beneath were hermetically sealed with cement on which were laid brown encaustic tiles . . . The plastered ceiling was taken down and replaced by a panel roof of pitch pine'.

The organ, which had stood in the gallery, was moved to its position north of the chancel. This organ has been bought by subscribers in 1828. Before then, psalms and hymns had been sung by a group, accompanied by a variety of instruments, all positioned in the gallery. When the hymn had been announced, a red curtain was drawn across the gallery, hiding the performers from view. 'Nevertheless' she writes 'those of the congregation whose seats faced the East, always turned round to the gallery when the singing began'. At about this time the right of way through the church tower was closed after 700 years.

The tanning industry, so long a staple of the town, was now discontinued and Mr Richard Foster gave his tannery market and sale room to the Church to serve as a Sunday School.

In 1884 universal Parliamentary suffrage for men was finally achieved. Lostwithiel Borough Council was not reformed, however, until 1885 when, following a petition to the Privy Council, signed by nearly 200 local people, the town was grangted a new charter and the old Corporation was formally abolished. The new charter provided for a Council of 12 persons elected from not less than 21 candidates. The freely elected Councillors were to choose a Mayor from among their number, and elect four Aldermen, not of their number.

On 2 November 1885 the election took place. 238 votes were cast from a total of 280 on the Electoral Roll. The candidates stood as 'Churchmen' or 'Dissenters', and six of each were elected. Mr Foster was elected Mayor. On Sunday 15 November 'the whole new Corporation attended by two Sergeants at Mace, came to the Morning Service, according to the ancient and invariable custom' (Hext).

For many years through the 19th century there had been an annual burlesque known as 'Mock Mayor Choosing' held in the same week as Mayor Choosing. Four men were drawn in a car escorted by two mock constables. All were masked, wore long noses, and were quite unrecognisable. A halt was made at each street corner and mock officials were elected. Every man was given a role: Mayor, Recorder, even 'down as low as hangman'. Then 'The Calendar' was read out — an account of all the transgressions of public figures over the past year. Written in satirical verse, this was an occasion to display wit, express derision and vent spleen. It is said to have degenerated into coarseness, which was the reason often given for the eventual demise of the custom. But the following poem would indicate other reasons: Address delivered at the Royal Talbot Hotel. At a dinner given to mark the disuse of the ancient ceremony of Mock Mayor Choosing — 23rd November 1886.

'Once more my late mock burgesses, around the board we meet
Drawn by an unexpected call from our self sought retreat
And though unlike our older feasts, this is a gift unearned
We've done it justice and our thanks are heartily returned
Since the old Corporation's gone with all its empty fuss
And better growth usurps its place, there is no need for us
To keep our yearly carnival in this enfranchised town
And hold removed abuses up, that we may run them down
Ye bolder few who bore the brunt, your occupations gone,
No more to mount the civic car your quaint disguise you'll don
Nor from your torch illumined height will fling your taunts and jeers
To gratify the broader tastes or shock more modest ears.
No more ye men who held the shafts and led the shouting throng
From Bunkers Hill to Royal Oak you'll haul our car along
Ye crier who with loud "Oyez" proclaiming went before
Yours was a most important part and hardest to give o'er
For you within the good Mayor's door received the brimming bowl
And from our subjects willing hands drew their accustomed toll.
(But ah! the toll we levied then and in a supper ate
Now goes into the hungry bag that holds the borough rate!)
Our clerk who kept the calendar, that catalogue of crime,
Plays the detective now no more but has a restful time
And we who did the unseen part in secrecy at home
(Of whom just 3 are with us here, and one's at Illfracombe)
No more we'll scoff at Council feasts nor sentence folk to gaol
Nor satire peaceful citizens nor at our rulers rail
We'll blacken paper never more for choosing of mock mayor
We ceased when 12 elected men stood around the civic chair
Now all who kept the custom up through good and ill renown
Your old support you have withdrawn and let it totter down
Its time is past, its turn is served, in ruin let it lie
We know not those who saw its birth, we all have seen it die.'

So the old order changeth . . . although during the 19th century Lostwithiel had seen the County Courts moved to Bodmin, the end of the tin coinage and the tanning industry, the sale of the Duchy buildings and the loss of jurisdiction over the River Fowey, by the end of the century the town was enjoying vastly improved communications and public services, and steady employment for its people. The men were experiencing the effects of the legislation which entitled them all to a role in the democratic government of both their town and country; women still had to wait a while longer for this.

The miners wear a curious woollen dress, with a cap like
this:  and the dress thus:  and they generally
have a candle stuck in front of the cap.

ABOVE: Sketches of miners by HM Queen Victoria in 1846, from *Leaves from the Journal of Our Life in the Highlands*. (RA) CENTRE: Interior of St Bartholomew's Church, 1822, possibly drawn by Lawrance. (LM) BELOW: St Faith's Convent, designed by G. E. Street, 1864. (DB)

ABOVE: The Convocation Hall undergoing alterations 1876-79 (prison on left), and BELOW: after alterations (with shop beyond). (Both DB)

ABOVE: Original pump, still in corner of old tannery yard, now Mr Ryan Rowe's garden. (RR) (IF) BELOW: North Street 1880s; first Bank Chapel at top of street, town houses on right. (RFE-C)

ABOVE: The railway came to Lostwithiel in 1859, (broad gauge). (DB)
CENTRE: Old broad gauge carriage, later used as a store in the Station yard, 1922. (CB) BELOW: The wooden station building survived until 1981. (V&AM)

ABOVE: Milltown Viaduct before 1896, a wooden structure on stone pillars. (LM) BELOW: Railway staff, c1900. (DT)

LEFT: Edgcumbe House, leased as shops in the 1890s. (FMH) (RIC)
RIGHT: Four generations of the Talling family c1900; this shop is now the North Street Dairy. (MH&PD) CENTRE: The Town shoot, called St Cadock's shoot in the 19th century. (IF) BELOW: 1890: Lady Fortescue (not in the picture) laid the foundation stone of the Working Men's Institute. (DB)

ABOVE: Cottages on Bodmin Hill, c1900. (RK) BELOW: Avery House, Bodmin Hill, c1900. (RK)

Cattle Market in Queen Street, and new Bank Chapel under construction, 1900. (RevFS)

Within Living Memory

In the pubs and clubs of Lostwithiel people enjoy sharing memories. Grandparents pass on tales they heard from their grandparents, which go back into the 19th century.

In 1980 the late F. Leslie Mayell, a teacher and Mayor of Lostwithiel in 1974, recorded a talk he had with Odessa Tomlin of North Street, about the past.

Born Odessa Short, at 6 Duke Street in 1892, she remembered three wars. She remembered the soldiers marching away up Nomansland Hill to the Boer War and the free tea in the Parade, to celebrate the relief of Mafeking.

She remembered the 1914-18 War, when she worked as a relief postman 'pushing a handcart with the midday post to the railway station'. Her two brothers enlisted, and Odessa knew the 21 Lostwithiel men who lost their lives.

Odessa's memory took her back much further, for she had a clear recall of her mother's stories of her youth. Odessa's mother had been born in Goosey Town in 1868. On one occassion Leslie Mayell read to Odessa an article written in 1871 about Goosey Town (the nickname then given to the cottages below the lime kilns). The article had described it as 'a poor miserable wretched looking hamlet. The houses . . . are approaching collapse . . . Within they are dirty, comfortless and dank . . . sometimes there is an unseemly mixture of the sexes, all huddled together in the same sleeping room . . . no wonder we have so much immorality among us . . . The drains are all open . . . reeking refuse is thrown upon the dunghill or into the cesspool hard by'. Odessa's reaction to the article was 'That's wrong, it makes it out worse than a slum, but it wasn't'.

Odessa's grandfather, George Burton, was born in Goosey Town in 1928, when the cottages were new. They were built to house bargemen and sawyers who worked in the saw mills on the common (now Coulson Park). George Burton had been a sawyer. The name Goosey Town arose because geese were kept on the common beyond. Odessa's grandfather had had a garden and probably kept a pig. Most families had a barrel of salted pilchards for the winter, which cost 1d for 12.

There was no sanitation; everything went into the river. Odessa's mother was the 11th child; her grandmother died having a 13th. As the children grew up they went into service. 'They had to make room for others coming along . . . They didn't bother about schooling . . . My grand mother had all her children christened so there must have been a sense of what was right and proper'.

As far back as anyone can remember there has, until recently, always been a garage in North Street. The original Mr Skelton set up in business in 1823 as a wheelwright, and agrricultural implement manufacturer. Bill Skelton made the original 'Butterfly' plough which moved the share laterally. This won a gold medal at the Crystal Palace in the 1880s. Skelton's made their own 'penny farthing' bicycles and pioneered 'safety cycles', making the chains link by link, by hand. The firm moved with the times into the motor car business, and were the sole agents in the area for Ford cars, around 1911-12 when the 'Tin Lizzie' cost about £150.

In the early 1930s Spencer Brown, who had started as an apprentice in 1909, became a partner in the business, and later the proprietor, until he retired in 1962. Spencer Brown served on the Borough Council for many years and was Mayor. He was a County Councillor and County Magistrate.

Living in the town are fourth generation descendants of Richard Walkham. Born in 1850, a fireman for 50 years, He was thought to be the oldest active volunteer in England when he died at the age of 76. A man of strong and colourful personality, Richard (known as Dick) led a vigorously active life, joining in otter hunts until the end. He worked for many years in the GWR workshops, and was the gravedigger and organ blower at St Bartholomew's. Dick regularly took part in the Mock Mayor Choosing and had many a good tale to tell. After a hard day's work he would walk to Bodmin to take part in a boxing match, striding home again after the bout. He was renowned as the 'Boxing Blacksmith'. All Lostwithiel attended the funeral of this much-loved and respected man.

Dick's daughter-in-law Kate, who was born on the same day as HM Queen Elizabeth the Queen Mother, proved her courage in the 1930s when her house on the Moors caught fire one morning. The three youngest of her eight children were in their bedroom. Kate went twice into the inferno and brought them to safety. Mrs Malah Rundle was one of these.

In 1907, 'the Common' was developed into a park by the generosity of Dr Nathaniel Thomas Coulson of San Francisco. Dr Coulson, born in Penzance in 1853, was apprenticed to a farmer at Penquite Farm, Lostwithiel at the age of seven years. When he was old enough, he enlisted in the Royal Navy and travelled around the world, settling down eventually in San Francisco. He became a dentist, invested his income in property, and grew rich. Always he carried with him memories of Lostwithiel, and in particular, memories of Miss Abigail Santo, a Sunday School teacher who had befriended him when he was a lonely little boy.

In 1906 Nathaniel lost all his property in the San Francisco earthquake, but Lostwithiel got its park, for Nathaniel started again and built another fortune.

A later project for Lostwithiel was to build a footbridge over the river to make accessible a piece of land, which by tradition belonged to the town. There were strong objections to this scheme by the owner of Lanwithan. Dr Coulson did not take 'No' easily, but the bridge was never built. Dr Coulson donated nine gold links to the Mayoral chain, he provided money for the Red Cross during the 1914-18 War, and established an Emigration Fund to help local young men to emigrate to America.

In 1906 a group of nine local agriculturists bought a plot of land off North Street and established the Lostwithiel Cattle Market Ltd. Markets were held monthly, then fortnightly, until 1973 when business was transferred to St Austell. The Market, convenient for the Railway Station, was a great improvement on the Queen Street Market. But as motor and rail traffic increased, the congestion caused on market days became intolerable, with animals, carts and motor cars trying to move in all directions through the town.

Many are the memories of those days: the sounds of the auctioneers' calls, the drovers' shouts, the bellowing and snorting of animals, the honking horns and screeching brakes, the clanking railway wagons and hissing steam engines, and the smells!

Years ago farmers would pay young boys 6d to drive their cows from the Market to the station yard. Eileen Redmond, living in North Street, watched from the safety of her bedroom, as huge bulls were led along blindfold. Cows crossing the bridge occasionally leapt into the river. During the war young evacuees from London, fascinated by the cows, would dodge round the pens to find mothers and calves, and try to squeeze milk into match boxes.

There were always many butchers' shops in Lostwithiel; in 1889 there were eleven; in the 1930s there were five, and almost as many slaughterhouses. One was in the Shire Hall, now the Palace Printers, and there was another 'killing house' near the station, from which lamb was sent regularly up country between May and September.

Children could spend the pennies they earned in the sweetie shops kept by ladies in their front rooms. Those with a 'heavy thumb' on the scales soon gained a reputation with their young customers.

The 1914-18 War changed life for everyone. Soldiers were billeted on householders, and many local men joined up. Women took over men's jobs and kept things going for four years. There was a soup kitchen in the old Grammar School. Desmond Thethewey tells of the day he ventured in and sampled the soup. Very good it was too, but hardly worth his Grannie's anger when she learned where he had been.

Every Saturday Desmond's grandad, the stoker in the Fire Brigade, prepared fresh sticks and paper for the steam pump engine, while Desmond polished the brass. School, on Bodmin Hill, he remembers as strict but fair. There were a few 'toughies' who challenged authority, but Mr Green would always get the better of them.

There was hardship after the war for those families who had lost fathers and sons. It was difficult too for young people to find work. Many left town to try elsewhere. Several young men joined the RAF, a new and glamorous service. Desmond's widowed mother refused to sign his papers, so he had to find work at home.

His employment pattern is probably typical of many men of his generation. He served an apprenticeship as a motor mechanic at Skelton's, but after this, the pay was so low he 'went jobbing'. He delivered milk, gardened, moved furniture and, by keeping busy all day, made a living. For a while he had to work away. Later in the 1930s he was lucky to get a job as an RAC patrol man, working between Bridgend and Dobwalls crossroads. He was provided with a push-bike, a uniform and a monthly salary.

After war service with the RAF, Desmond worked for the railway until the workshops closed. He travelled to the St Austell workshops for a while, then found employment at the Creamery, where he stayed until retirement. He served too on the Borough Council and worked hard for the town he loves.

Women proved their worth during the First War, and won some voting rights in 1917, but it was not until 1928 that there was universal suffrage at 21.

One young man to realize the importance of this was Sydney Brewer, who sought election to the Council. Sydney at the age of 90, recalled with a chuckle, that being a baker and starting work early, his afternoons were free. These he put to good use, canvassing the ladies and romped home at the election. Sydney was three times Mayor and was proud to be made a Freeman of the Town, as was his good friend Wilfred Jeffery. He was proud also of his family, and especially of his air hostess granddaughter Pat Kerr, who was awarded an MBE in 1990 for the work she did to establish the Shreepur Orphanage in Bangladesh.

The Lostwithiel Creamery employed local people for nearly 60 years between 1932-91. Set up by Nestlé, it changed hands several times. It became a mik-drying unit in 1959. Between 1983-85 its capacity was increased four-fold, by the erection of a large drying tower. This was out of scale with the town, and caused much controversy but, as it created more work, it was accepted. By 1990 this efficient new unit was redundant. The tower has now been dismantled, and it is as through it never were.

Electric power was brought to Lostwithiel in 1936. The new Co-op, on the corner of Fore Street and Queen Street, was the first shop in town to be lit by electricity. The take-up of this new amenity was not immediate. Property owners, especially those who had shares in the Gas Company, were not so eager.

That same year, 1936, the compulsory driving test was introduced, and Christine Barnicoat was the first lady driver in Lostwithiel to take the test; she passed. One of the first local ladies to drive a car was Mrs Ruby Watts, then Miss Beavis, who was a familiar figure in the early 1920s, driving her primrose yellow Austin 7 with a black top.

Until 1939 the main route through Lostwithiel was over the bridge and along North Street, reputedly the narrowest main road between Lands End and John O'Groats. The need for a by-pass was urgent, but several buildings had to be demolished first. The loss of the Royal Talbot Hotel, a coaching inn and venue for balls, concerts and dinners for over 100 years, caused most distress. Buildings at the other end of Queen Street also had to go.

The new Liddicoat Road, incorporating bridges over the railway and the river, brought great relief to the town. Now in 1993 the railway bridge is being replaced, and the river bridge strengthened to comply with EEC regulations, in order to carry 40-ton lorries. The town is outraged, and a petition against such traffic has been sent to the County Council. Heavy vehicles approaching from St Austell have several times gone out of control and careered into the shops at the bottom of the hill, causing much damage and on one occasion, death and serious injuries.

In 1991 spirits were raised by proposals for an alterntive route to St Austell from the east, which would have relieved Lostwithiel of through-traffic. However, these proposals met with opposition elsewhere and the County Council is now struggling to find a satisfactory solution to the problem. Lostwithiel has its own traffic problems, it provides free car parks, but garaging is scarce, and its ancient streets are often choked with cars.

The new Fire Station was opened in 1992. Fire fighting has been organised in Lostwithiel for 300 years. In 1650 one of the church bells, designated 'the fire bell', summoned able-bodied citizens to man the fire buckets. The manual fire pump given by Lord Edgcumbe in 1761 was replaced in 1804 by a horse-drawn bucket-fed pump. A hundred years later a steam fire engine was commissioned. Once, attending a farm fire where water was unattainable, cider was pumped to quell the flames. Throughout the Second World War, a trailer pump, towed by a lorry from Skelton's Garage, was used by the volunteers (by then part of the National Fire Service), particularly during the Plymouth blitz.

County re-organization cost Lostwithiel its Fire Service in 1952, until 1969 when it was reinstated. Retained Station B17 was opened in Bodmin Hill under the leadership of Sub-Officer Roger Pascale, who would have been proud today to see the new station in the capable hands of Station Officer Vic May.

For over 20 years, the Glyn Cinema on South Street was a popular rendezvous. Built by Mr Henry Williams on a corner of the Old Shire Hall complex, it was opened in 1937. There was a competition to choose a name for it, and the prize was free entry to one show a week, for a year.

Des Talling started work as a projectionist on his 14th birthday in 1937. Only twice can he recall it being closed. At the outbreak of war it closed for a week, while staff learned to deal with incendiary bombs. On 26 November 1954 there was no show for the cinema was flooded. It was the day before Des's wedding, and his bride Eileen, in North Street, was carrying all her wedding presents upstairs to safety; North Street was flooded too. The Glyn closed down in 1960, owing to the counter-attractions of TV, Mr Williams converted it into a house, and he and his wife live there in retirement.

In 1928 Lostwithiel built its first Council houses at St George's Park, and developed other estates over the years. In 1962 the ancient mill at Tanhouse Lane was demolished and flats built there for the elderly. The Old Grammar School, unused for many years, suffered the same fate in 1981, and was replaced by pensioners' flats, built by the Devon & Cornwall Housing Association behind the Georgian facade.

The Second World War brought great activity. Into town came 'the troops' — British, American, Javanese and others. Lanwithan, Boconnoc and Pill were taken over; the soldiers and sailors camped in the grounds. The Americans set up a laundry in Coulson Park. Military Police kept order, and were as familiar in the streets as the local 'bobby'. The cinema was full and dances crowded, choral and drama societies flourished, and 'forces' swelled the congregations of church and chapel. The Americans laid an extra railway siding by the station, and residents became used to the continual clanking, day and night, as wagonloads of supplies were delivered and distributed. Among these were thousands of shells, which were stored alongside the Liskeard-St Austell road in Nissen huts a few yards apart, for mile upon mile.

A Scotsman, who regularly drove tankers in convoy through Lostwithiel for the RAF, remembers a motherly lady who had a roadside café here and served the drivers scrambled eggs; they called her 'Lostwithoutya'.

Through 1940-41 evacuees arrived regularly from London. Doreen Brown (then Newman) was five years old when she left home to set off from Paddington Station, on an eight hour journey into the unknown. Arriving here tired and bewildered, the little ones were taken to the school, and from there to their billets to meet their foster parents. Doreen has been close to the Pearce family ever since.

Country life was totally strange to the young Londoners. Some of them pined for home; a few were so homesick they even set off to walk to London along the railway track. Fortunately there were picked up alongside the Creamery. Most settled own happily. The schools were bursting at the seams, and the Bank and Wesley Sunday Schools were taken over as extra classrooms. Among the evacuees were Roman Catholics; as there was no church for them here, the Church Rooms were lent for their worship.

Odessa Tomlin once again helped the 'war effort'. She and her husbnd ran a home at Springfields, Bridgend, for evacuees who were taken ill, caring for them until they were better. Seven of the evacuees are still here, their grandchildren now second generation Cornish.

Later in the war, Italian and German prisoners of war, many not yet twenty, were brought into the area and worked on the farms.

Lostwithiel Home Guard dealt with a Dornier aircraft, shot down over Boconnoc. Forty years later three unexploded bombs from that aircraft were discovered and detonated.

As D-Day approached, convoys of tanks and trucks passed through Lostwithiel, picking up the soldiers and the shells as they went, and the town was left, suddenly quiet and empty.

After 1945 life settled down. Every year the town pays its respects to those of two wars who gave their lives. The Church is always full for the Civic Service of Remembrance.

Change since the war has been gradual, but fundamental. Secondary education was moved to Fowey, giving the children greater opportunities, but it was a loss to the town.

At first there was work for everyone, but there has been a decline over the years. When railway maintenance work was moved from Lostwithiel in the 1950s, job opportunities for skilled men were lost.

After this, the increasing use of the motor car changed life-styles, and more people were able to travel to other towns to work and shop, which brought about the demise of many small local businesses. The ironmongers, jewellers and furnishers have gone. Lostwithiel is no longer self-sufficient as it once was. However, a number of specialist shops now attract people to come here.

In 1968 Lostwithiel lost its Borough status. Although it retains its Mayor and Town Council and some local powers, it is not now completely master of its fate. It is part of Restormel Borough.

Restormel was responsible for building Lostwithiel's sewage treatment works in 1974. This is currently about to be updated and extended to cope with a possible growth in population of up to 3,500.

Horse-drawn wagonnette driven by Mr Frank Secombe, jobmaster at Royal Talbot Hotel stables, 1905. (LM)

There are many 'new people' in Lostwithiel, replacing as of old, those who have moved on. The town is friendly and courteous to its newcomers, absorbing willingly those who feel comfortable here, and want to be part of the community.

1989 was the year the town celebrated the 800th anniversary of its first charter. The highlight was the visit of HM the Queen and HRH Prince Philip on 9 June. The inspected the original charter of 1189 and the civic regalia. Her Majesty told the Town Clerk, Fran Dennision, that she was the first lady Town Clerk she had met.

Memorable among all the celebrations, which went on throughout the year, were the Medieval Market Day organized by the Chamber of Commerce, and the Pageant of History written by Gwen Powell Jones and staged at Restormel Castle, with a cast of over 100 Lostwithiel people. The town was proud to host the Cornish Gorsedd that year. Almost all the residents were involved in the special activities of 1989 in one way or another, demonstrating clearly the civic pride and community spirit that exists here.

ABOVE: 1906: Charles Nicholls, telegraph boy (the present Mayor's uncle) was to be awarded the Military Medal for bravery at Ypres during the First World War; standing outside Wm Wilce's shop, now Lostwithiel Stores. (WN) BELOW: The bridge 1905, old Toll House behind the sailor. (LM)

ABOVE: Fore Street, 1907. (DB) BELOW: Empire Day: 24 May 1908 — dedication of the new flagpole in Coulson Park. (LM)

ABOVE: Bodmin Hill in Edwardian days; little girls wear their 'pin befores'. (DB) BELOW: Aftermath of the flood, Queen Street, 1903. (DB)

ABOVE: Bridgend 1905, Reading Room on left and Bridgend Toll House facing the road. (DB) BELOW: Nomansland in Edwardian Days — cottages and Celtic Cross. (DB)

ABOVE: Volunteer Fire Brigade with horse-drawn steam pump engine, after 1904. (DT) BELOW: Chimney fire or practice at the old Talbot Hotel? After 1904. (RK) RIGHT: Richard Walkham, still a volunteer fireman when he died aged 76 in 1927. (MR)

ABOVE: TRH The Prince and Princess of Wales visit Restormel Castle in 1905; Lord Clifden is in the bowler hat on the left, Lady Clifden, centre and Hon Tommy (killed in action in 1915) on the right. (LM)
BELOW: Edwardian gentlemen of Lostwithiel; Oscar H. Jarrett on the right. Who were the others? (MES)

LEFT: Entrance to Restormel Iron Mine c1908, mine owner Oscar Henry Jarrett second from right. The mine closed down a year or two after this. (MES) BELOW: Industrial buildings at the mine surface, c1908. (MES) RIGHT: John Vincent, Town Crier, charged 1s 6d to carry messages around town, 2s 6d to include Bridgend. He lived in Victoria and joined up in 1914. (DB)

ABOVE: Bridgend, 1913. (DB) BELOW: Fun postcard, 1913; a strip of photographs is hidden under a flap. (DB)

ABOVE: Town Quay, 1910; limestone was barged upriver to the lime kilns. (LM) LEFT: Old lime kilns today. (IF) RIGHT: Bodmin Hill corner, c1910. (DB)

LEFT: Nathaniel Daniel (1789-1879), Lostwithiel's first letter-carrier. (MH) BELOW: 1917: Nathaniel Daniel's grandson, Cyril, and family. Cyril and his eldest son, Cyril, were both postmen in peacetime. Standing by father's knee are Adrian and Edris (Mrs Gardener). (V&AM) RIGHT: Royal Oak Hotel, 1920; parts of the building date back to medieval times. (LM)

ABOVE: Odessa Tomlin (née Short) on right with parents, sister and three soldiers billeted with them at 6, Duke Street in 1915. (DT)
BELOW: Bodmin Hill School staff, 1922; standing L to R: Miss Dora Nicholls, F. A. Green (HM), Mrs Green, Miss A. M. Neal, sitting: Miss Kate Nicholls, Joseph Levers, Mrs S. Harris. (LM)

BLOTTER

KEEP THIS AS A USEFUL BLOTTER AND AS A REMINDER THAT OUR VALUE IS UNEQUALLED.

The Oak Suite shown will lend charm and distinction to your Bedroom. Ask to see it!

The "DERWENT" Suite in rich Oak combines distinction with *real* economy. 4ft. Wardrobe with rods and hooks, etc. £6 . 11 . 6. 3ft. 3in. Low Dressing Chest with frameless mirrors £4 . 2 . 0. 2ft. 6in. 3-drawer Chest £2 . 6 . 0.
4ft. 6in. Bedstead to match 39/6. **£12 . 19 . 6.**

ALFRED JULIAN,
Complete House Furnisher,
LOSTWITHIEL & LOOE.

ABOVE: Blotter advertising Julian's furniture shop in the 1920s, now the Tawny Owl and Kitchen Garden. (JB&MO) BELOW: 1st Lostwithiel Girl Guides, 1926; Christine Barnicoat fourth from left. (CB)

ABOVE: Meet in Monmouth Square, 1926. (DB) BELOW: North Street, always liable to flooding, Skelton's Garage on the left, 1928. (LM)

ABOVE: The Creamery opened in 1933, a fleet of vans at the ready.
(LM) BELOW: Creamery staff 1938. (LM)

Telephone: Lostwithiel **26**.

W. J. WHERRY
Garage Proprietor.

MOTOR - CYCLE, Cycle and General Repairer.
(Any Make Supplied).

CARS FOR HIRE.
PETROL, OILS, &c., STOCKED.

Queen Street, Lostwithiel

LEFT: Duke Street 1930s. (DB) BELOW: W. J. Wherry advertised in the Lostwithiel guide book in the 1930s. (RK) RIGHT: The Glyn Cinema (1937-1960) and CENTRE: The projectors. (Both D&ET) BELOW: Slaughter house winch, still at Palace Printers. (CPB)

ABOVE: Royal Talbot Hotel, demolished to make way for the new road in 1939, (DB) and BELOW: the replacement, built on the site of the stables, the 19th century Wesleyan Chapel beyond. (CSL)

ABOVE: The new Restormel bridge carries the by-pass road over the river, 1939. (CSL) BELOW: 1939 Hospital helpers met weekly at Cowbridge to make up bandages, their materials bought with the proceeds of a 1d a week fund. (LM)

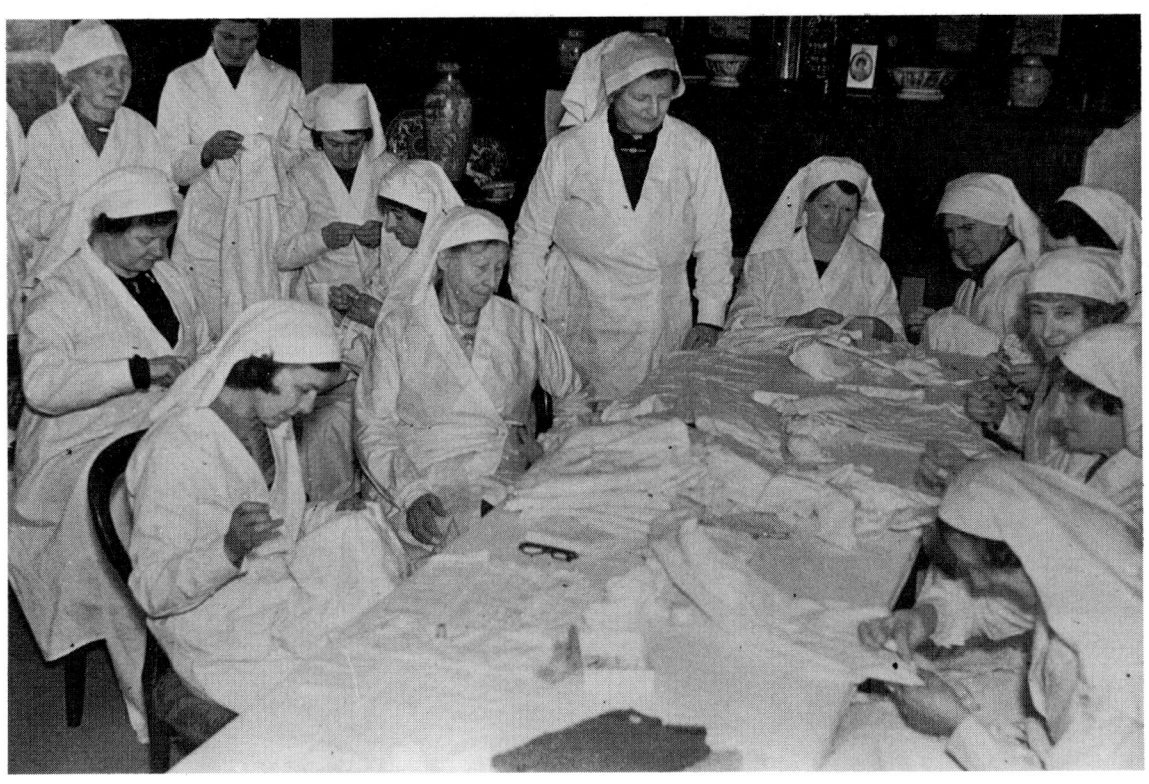

ABOVE: Evacuees arrive 16.7.41 — Ian Addington, 8 years 9 months and Ronald Brown, 7 years 5 months settle in with Mrs Ashton at 12, Robartes Terrace. (D&RB) BELOW: Mothers and babies evacuated from Plymouth, with Councillors and volunteer helpers. (D&RB)

ABOVE: A party for Javanese sailors stationed at Pill. (LM) BELOW: Spencer Brown inspects the Home Guard. (LM)

ABOVE: Mrs Brown brings gifts of sweets from South America, to pupils at Bodmin Hill School, 1942. (LM) BELOW: Beating the Bounds 1950, Lady Howe on horseback bending to greet a friend; once an annual custom, now held less frequently. (CB)

ABOVE: July 1950, TM George VI and Queen Elizabeth visit Lostwithiel. (V&AM) INSET: Privileged customers watch the Royal progress from Vida Carter's shop window (ladies' outfitters, now Bragg's Antiques). (V&AM) BELOW: Lostwithiel Silver Band marches under the celebratory arch. (LM)

ABOVE: *The Cornish Riviera passes through Lostwithiel* — a painting by Don Breckon. (© DonB, owned by JS&JW) BELOW: *The Fowey Rattler* en route for Fowey, Milltown viaduct in background — by Don Breckon. (© DonB, owned by I&CK)

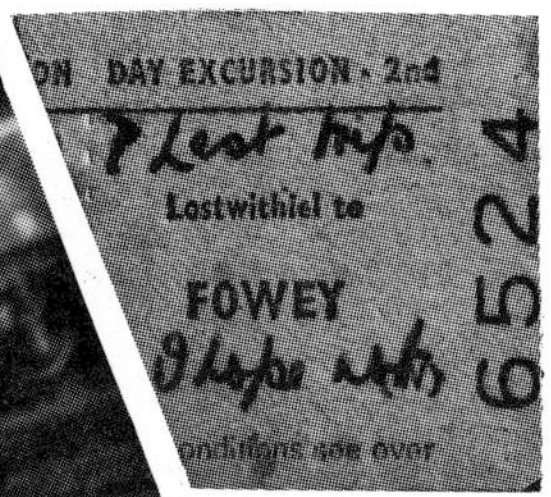

ABOVE: Leslie Gardener, shunter and Stan May, signalman 40 years ago. (V&AM) RIGHT: Souvenir of a sentimental journey; Doris Liddicoat travelled on the last passenger train to Fowey, 12.1.65. (DL) (IF) BELOW: Skiffle in the Globe Inn; 'The Globe Trotters' broadcast with Wilfred Pickles in *Have a Go* in 1958. (D&RB)

ABOVE: Charles Day rehearses St Bartholomew's choir, 1960s. Charles was Choirmaster and Organist for nearly 30 years, then served as Organist at Boconnoc for a further 20 years after retirement. (CD)
BELOW: A cartoon by choirboy Derek Parker, 1967. (CD)

ABOVE: Building defences against flooding, 1960s. (CPB) BELOW: Strengthening foundations of the bridge, 1970s. (CPB)

ABOVE: Mrs de Lancey Nicholls retires as President of the Lostwithiel Old Cornwall Society, 1982; L to R: Margaret Hurrell, Esme Santo, Dorothy de Lancey Nicholls, Christine Barnicoat and Douglas Gabriel. (CPB) BELOW: Children representing their schools bring information for a Time Capsule to be buried in foundations of the Community Centre, 1982; adults L to R: Rex Stephens, Sydney Brewer, Jonathan Barker. (CPB)

ABOVE: For many years Miss Olive Osborne cared for the swans. (CPB)
LEFT: Miss Nellie Tom (1907-86), Aunt Nell to generations of school children, and a familiar figure at her cottage door for many years. (IF)
RIGHT: Mrs Mary Charity Brewer cuts her 100th birthday cake, watched by Betty and Walter Strong, her daughter and son-in-law, 1986. (CPB)

ABOVE: The Great Western Industrial Village in the old GWR workshops, after the fire of 1987. (IF) BELOW: In 1987 three shops were destroyed by a runaway lorry. (V&AM)

Here and Now

Over the years many organisations have come and gone, meeting the needs and interests of the people. Among the oldest still flourishing are the local Lodge of Freemasons, the Lostwithiel Silver Band founded in 1922, and the Women's Institute, which has been active since 1924. The Women's Branch of the British Legion, the Scouts, Cubs, Guides and Brownies and the St John Ambulance Brigade all have long histories and are important in the town. The Garden Society, founded during the 1939-45 War, currently has about 70 members. For 27 years the Pre-School Playgroup has been strongly supported. The Conservative Club was one of the last four in the country to remain an all-male bastion. Not until 1990 were women members admitted, and then without voting rights.

The town has long been interested in sport. The Bowls Club dates back to 1927. The King George VI playing field, acquired in the early 1950s, improved opportunities for football and other sports, making up for the loss of a playing field when the new road was built in 1939. River fishing is a popular pastime.

The Golf and Country Club is a new amenity for the town. The golf course is set in beautiful surroundings, and there are the added attractions of a swimming pool and tennis courts.

The Community Centre was opened ten years ago; its tremendous success over the years is a tribute to the people who put so much effort into getting the project started, and seeing it through to completion. Lostwithiel Town Council bought the land and gave the Memorial Fund to help initially, but the bulk of the money to build the Centre was raised by the personal efforts of the people who believed in the concept. It is run by the Community Association and caters for everyone from toddlers to pensioners; the staff is always busy. The Centre provides facilities for clubs, concerts, markets, parties, and a variety of indoor sporting activities, including squash. The Lostwithiel Faith Assembly meets here each Sunday. Everyone looks forward to the monthly newsletter produced by the Association. The Tourist Information Office is in the Centre, and early breakfasts are provided for visitors on Saturday mornings during the holiday season.

In the summer, as a result of the hard work of the Britain in Bloom Committee and enthusiastic householders, the town is bright with flowers. The Lostwithiel Silver Band and the Lostwithiel Brass 88 both play on high days and holidays.

Important in the calendar of events are Mayor Making Sunday, the Carnival, the Regatta, Remembrance Sunday and the Christmas Pageant, traditions old and not so old. Lostwithiel has been twinned with Pleyber Christ in Britanny since 1979. Many good and lasting friendships have been made, and visits are exchanged regularly.

There are about 40 different societies and clubs active in Lostwithiel. A local branch of the Royal National Lifeboat Institution is being set up in 1993: the first Fowey lifeboat came by rail to Lostwithiel in 1859, the year the railway was opened. From here it sailed down to Fowey and round to its base at Polkerris. It was a 30ft six-oared boat called *The Catherine Rashleigh*.

The Lostwithiel Players has recently been founded in memory of Burness Bunn, a well-loved local journalist, poet and playwright who died in 1990. There are a number of talented writers, musicians, artists and craftsmen and women living and working here.

Lostwithiel was one of the first towns in Cornwall to take conservation and recycling seriously. The 'paper mountains' and 'recycling banks', organized by Richard Bower and his 'green network' colleagues, led the way.

Longevity and Lostwithiel go hand in hand. Four residential homes care for the elderly, WRVS deliver Meals on Wheels and serve at the Luncheon Club. Hillyar, once the town house of the Kendals, now has a role as part of the Care in the Community programme.

The Lostwithiel Museum was opened in 1971 in the old Corn Market and Town Gaol. The Corn Market had served for a long time as the Fire Station, and the town's first fire engine is a museum exhibit. The museum was pioneered by Mrs Dorothy De Lancey Nicholls, Miss Esme Santo, and Mr Eric Furse, together with other members of the Lostwithiel Old Cornwall Society, who worked hard to bring it into being. It is now run independently. All the exhibits have been given by local people, and it is funded entirely by donations. The energetic Museum Committee is looking to the future. Members are making detailed studies of various aspects of the town's history, which they plan to present in a readily accessible form.

Lostwithiel is a caring community. Money is raised constantly for a host of causes, by direct giving and by organized functions. People are generous with their time and talents.

The Chamber of Commerce fundraises and sponsors many events for the benefit of the whole town, and it is always looking to improve employment and trading opportunities.

The development of the Great Western Industrial Village in the old GWR workshops has brought a variety of small businesses. There are others making use of small-scale premises which are ideal sites for new technology. It is hoped that the redundant Creamery site will also be used to create work.

Lostwithiel is well known for its shops. Its antique shops, fairs and auctions attract collectors through the year. Here are paintings, pottery, fine lace, hand-spun wools, old and new books, and every sort of music on tape and CD.

Lostwithiel finds itself increasingly involved in tourism. This presents a challenge; maintaining that fine balance, whereby visitors are made truly welcome and yet the character of the town is kept intact.

There is probably now more public awareness and active concern about the development of the town, than ever before. This promises well for the future for, despite all the wider constraints, the quality of life will be determined by those who choose to live and work in this proud and ancient town.

ABOVE: Lostwithiel's three lady Mayors, L to R: Doris Liddicoat 1956-58, Ida Keast 1986-88 and Gwen Powell-Jones 1983-86. (JB) BELOW: Centenary celebrations 1989; HM the Queen signs a photograph of herself in the Mayor's Parlour. (JB)

INSET: Programme for the 1989 Pageant, designed by Don Breckon. LEFT: Robert Cardinham, Lord of Restormel and his Lady canter up to their castle; (JB) while ABOVE: citizens of the future take part in this pageant of the past. (JB) BELOW LEFT: Mistress Jude Martelli, stallholder at the medieval market. (MW) BELOW: Lostwithiel hosts the Cornish Gorsedd in 1989. (JB)

LEFT: Stephen Peareth with his prize-winning pumpkins, Lostwithiel Garden Society Show, 1992. (CPB) RIGHT: Gordon Faddy of Lostwithiel, well known fund-raiser for Churchtown Farm Recreation and Education Centre (Spastics' Society). (JB) BELOW: Loswithiel Volunteer Fire Brigade outside the Station on the newly named Pleyber Christ Way, 1993. (IF)

The end and a beginning — ABOVE: dismantling the milk drying tower in 1991; Fire Station Officer Vic May was 'bleeped' immediately after taking this picture: fire in the tower. Smoke is just discernible between the chimneys. (V&AM) BELOW: The Cubs enjoy their new HQ a-building on the site of the old Cattle Market. (CPB)

Bibliography

Barton, Rita M. (Ed) *Life in Cornwall at the end of the 19th Century,* D. Bradford Barton, 1974
   Life in Cornwall in the late 19th Century, D. Bradford Barton, 1972
Bennett, Alan *Cornwall through the mid 19th Century,* Kingfisher Railway Productons, 1987
Boger Rev Canon *Lostwithiel Bridge and Its Memories* 1887
Borlase, Wm'. *Antiquities of Cornwall,* First Edition 1754; EP Publishing, 1973
Brown, H. M. *The Church in Cornwall,* Oscar Blackford Ltd, Truro 1964
   Battles Royal, Libra Books 1981
Carew, Richard *Survey of Cornwall,* 1602
Courtney, W. P. *The Parliamentary Representation of Cornwall,* Thomas Pettite & Co, London 1889
Chadwyck Healey, C.E.H. (Ed) *Sir Ralph Hopton's Narrative of his Campaign in the War 1642-44,* Somerset Records, Vol XVIII, 1902
Daniel, Rev J. J. (Ed T. Peters) *The History and Geography of Cornwall,* Netherton & Worth, Truro; Houlston & Sons, London, 1906
Foot, Andrew *History of St Veep Church and Parish, including Lerryn,* 1986
Gillespie, B. Guild *On Stormy Seas,* Horsdal & Schubart, Victoria BC, Canada, 1992
Hamilton Jenkin, A. K. *Cornwall and Its People,* David & Charles, 1945
Hatcher, John *Rural Economy & Society in the Duchy of Cornwall 1300 - 1500,* CUP, 1970
   English Tin Production & Trade before 1550, Clarendon Press, Oxford, 1973
Henderson, Charles, Ed A. L. Rowse & M. I. Henderson *Essays in Cornish History,* OUP, 1935
Hext, Frances Margery *Memorials of Lostwithiel and Restormel,* 1891
   Jean (Ed) *The Staniforth Diary,* D. Bradford Barton Ltd
Lewis, G. R. *The Stannaries,* D. Bradford Barton Ltd, 1908
Lyson *Britannia Magna – Cornwall,* 1813
McArthur *The River Fowey,* Cassell, 1947
Morris, John (Ed) *Domesday Book – Cornwall,* Phillimore, 1979
Nicholls, Dorothy de Lancey *The Black Prince*
   Lostwithiel, 1974
   Gleanings from a Cornish Notebook
Noall, Cyril *A History of Cornish Mail & Stage Coaches,* D. Bradford Barton
Norway, Arthur H. *Highways & Byways of Cornwall and Devon,* McMillan & Co, 1897
Pearse, Richard *The Ports and Harbours of Cornwall,* H. E. Warne Ltd, 1963
Platt, Colin *Medieval England,* Routledge & Kegan Paul, 1978
Polsue, Joseph *Lakes Parochial History of the County of Cornwall,* W. Lake, Truro, 1867; EP Publications Ltd, 1974
Probert, John C. C. *The Sociology of Cornish Methodism,* Cornish Methodist Historical Assoc, 1971
Rowse, A. L. *Tudor Cornwall,* McMillan, 1941
Shaw, Thomas *A History of Cornish Methodism,* D. Bradford Barton, 1967
Stockdale, F. W. L. *Excursions Through Cornwall,* Simpkin & Marshall, 1824
Seymour, W. H. *Restormel Castle,* 1911
Smith, Eleanor *Lostwithiel 1189-1989,* 1989
Trevelyan, G. M. *English Social History,* Longman, 1944
Whetter, James *Cornwall in the 17th Century – An Economic Survey,* Lodenek Press, 1974
Young, Denham *Richard of Cornwall,* Basil Blackwell, 1947

PAPERS

The Black Prince's Register *Part II 1351-65 Cornwall*
Cornish Archaeology No 14 – Irwin, Mary M. Article – *An Earthwork at Restmorel,* 1975
Corwall Census, 1851 – Vol 4, Part 2 – Lostwithiel, Pro Ref 110107, 1904
Minchinton, Walter (Ed) *Exeter Papers in Economic History No 12,* Univ of Exeter, 1979
Pounds, Norman, Paper – *The Social Structure of Lostwithiel in the early 19th Century,* 1979
   Paper – *The Duchy Palace Lostwithiel*
Radford, C. A. Ralegh *Restormel Castle Cornwall,* Ministry of Works, 1947
Thomas, Nigel & Buck, Colin *An Historical & Archaeological investigation of Restormel Castle, Cornwall:* an Interim Report, Cornwall County Council, 1993
Toy, Sidney *The Round Castles of Cornwall,* Society of Antiquaries, London, 1933

Lostwithiel Bridge, drawn by Ian Fraser.

Index

All figures in *italics* refer to illustrations

Aachen 23
Abraham Lestymour,
   tinner 31
Acts of Parliament 1540 ... 36
   Cornwall Railway Bill ... 74
   Reform 1832 54,65
   Supremacy 1534 35
   Turnpike 1751 65
   Weights & Measures
   1496 34
Accident (1987) *118*
Addington, Ian *108*
Addison, Joseph 53
Admiral of the River 33
American forces 88
Anniversary 800 .... *121*
Ann's Gallery 74
antique shops 120
Aquitaine 31
Arthur, Sarah 54
Ashton, Mrs *108*
Avery House *83*
Baldwin Fitz Turstin 15
Balfour, Sir Wm 45
Barcelona 16
Bardi Society 26
Barnicoat,
   Christine 87,*102,116*
Barker, Jonathan *116*
Bay of Biscay 16
Bayonne 16
Beating the Bounds *110*
Bertrand de Dinant 15
Black Death 29
Black Prince, 1st Duke of
   Cornwall .. 29,et seq, *32*,37
Blackmore 34
Bligh, Capt Wm 54
Boconnoc 11,33,43,45,
   51,*57*,73,88,89,*114*
Bodardle Manor
   (Bodarther) 12,15,18
Bodinnick 16,29,33
Bodmin 11,12,15,26,
   30,33,67,76,86
   Parkway 74
bordars 15
Bordeaux 16
Borlase 11
Bower, Richard 120
Braddock 43
   Church 43
   Down 11,43
Breckon, Don *112,122*
Brewer, Charity Mary ... *117*
   Sydney 87,*116*
bridges,
   Lostwithiel .. *72*,91,115,*132*
   Respryn 43,44
   Restormel (Baldwin's)
   .... 15*107*
Bridgend 67,73,*94,97,98*
Brittany 16
Bronscombe, Bishop ... 25,51
Bronze Age 11,12
Brown, Doreen 89
   Ron *108*
   Spencer 86,*109*
   Spencer, Mrs *110*
Bunn, Burness 120

Burnett, Joseph 66
Burton, George 85
Butterfly Plough 85
Calais, seige of 29
Camden 18
Camelford, Lord 67
Cardinham 15,16
   Andrew 18
   Castle *14*
   Robert 16,*122*
Care in the Community . 120
Carew, Richard 18,33,34,
   35,36,37
Carter, John, ARIBA 36
Carter's Vida shop *111*
Cartulary of Edmund 18,24
Castle Dore 11,12,*13*,45
   Lantyan 12
Catherine Rashleigh, The ... *119*
cattle market 74,*84*
Celtic cross *13*,94
Celts 12
census, 1841 73
   1851 73,74
Centaur 54
Charters
   Anniversary 89
   Dukedom of Cornwall
   1337 29
   Lostwithiel c1189 ..... 16,*20*
   1269 22,23
   1609 37
   1885 75
   tinners 1200 17
   1305 26
cCholera 74
churches and chapels
   Bank chapel ... 55,74,*79,84*
   Congregational 53
   Methodist 1993 ... 36,55,*64*
   Primitive Methodist 55
   St Bartholomew 16,*19*,
   35,45,56,66,86
   aisles 16,*19*,35
   alabaster carving *19*
   choir *114*
   font 28
   interior, 1822 77
   Patronal Feast Day 45
   recesses 16,*19*
   restoration 35,75
   tower 16,25,*28*
   St George
   altar stone *39*
   Chantry *39*
   St Nectan *13*,*42*,75
   St Saviour's Chapel . 54,55
   St Sampson 12
   United Free Methodist . 55
   Wesleyan 55,60,*106*
Church Rooms 89
Churchtown 12
   Farm, Spastic Society .. *124*
Cinque Ports 17
Cleveland, Earl of 45
Clifden, Viscounts 53,*96*
Cober river *10*,11,16,
   22,24,26,66
Cologne Bishhop of 23
Communion plate, 1775 .. *41*
Coombe, Matthew 26
Co-op 87
corn market 53,58,120

Cornish emblem
   17th cent *39*
   Gorsedd 90,*123*
Cornish Riviera 112
Cornwall County Courts .. 67
   Railway 74
   Railway Bill 1846 .... *74*
   Survey 1533-40 36
Coulson, Dr Nathaniel 86
   Park 85,88,92
Courts, Assize 24
   Augmentation 35
   Chancery 51
   County 24,25,29,76
   Hundred 24,29
   Maritime 29,33
   Martial 29
   Stannary 24,25,29
   Star Chamber 35
Courtney, Sir Hugh ... 33,51
   W.P. 53,54
Cowbridge 54,*107*
Creamery 87,89,120
   staff *104*
   vans *104*
Crecy, Battle of 29
Crusade 16
Curteys, Randolph 51
   Richard 35,51
   Tristan 51,56
Curtoys, Gerald 26
Dabernoun, John 30
Daniel, Adrian *100*
   Cyril & family *100*
   Edris *100*
   Nathaniel *100*
Dark Ages 12
Davies, Walter 66
Day, Charles *114*
D-Day 89
Dennison, Fran 90
deer park 25
Devon and Cornwall
   Housing Association 88
Digby, Col 44
Director 54
Discovery 52
Domesday Book 15
Doublebois Station 74
Dornier aircraft 89
Dower House 36,53
Duchy, estates 69,76
   Palace 24
Edgcumbe 36,53,88
   House *82*
   Richard, 1st Lord
   36,53,58
Edgcumbes 51,54,74
Edward-Collins, Richard
   Foster 54
Edmund,
   Earl of Cornwall . 24,25,33
Edwardian gentlemen *96*
Eltham, John of 25
Emigration Fund 86
Empire Day, 1908 92
English Clays L.P. Co Ltd ... 12
English Heritage 37
Essex, Earl of 43,44,53
evacuees 89,*108*
Evesham,
   Battle of Exeter 11
   exports, 12th cent 16

Faddy, Gordon *124*
Falmouth 65
fairs 25
Fawi, Port of 16,*18*,25
   Haven 29
   Waters of 16
Feodary 24
Fire Brigade 87,*95,124*
   station 88,120,*124*
flood, North Street 68
   prevention 115
   Queen Street 93
Fortescue, Hon George 52
   Lady *82*
Foster, Richard 65,66,75
Fosters 51,54
Fowey 16,24,34,*38*,
   43,44,45,89
   Harbour Board 33
   Life Boat 119
   river 11,12,15,22,31,
   44,76
   Town of 29,33,65
Fowey Rattler 112
Freemasons 119
Furse, Eric 120
Gabriel, Douglas *116*
Gardener, Edris *100*
   Leslie *113*
gas works 74
Genoa 16
German, electors 89
   POWs 89
Germany 23
Giants Hedge 11
Gillray, James 52
   cartoon 52,*57*
Globe Trotters *113*
Glyn Cinema 88,*105*
Golant 12,16,29,65
Goosey Town 85
Gorlois, Castle of 12
Gorsedd 1989 .... *122*
Gray, Lord Ruthin 43
Great Hall 24,25,34,44
Green, Mr Headmaster 87
Green, F.A. *101*
   Mrs *101*
Grenville, Richard 43,44
Grim 12,15
Guild Merchants 24
Guildhall 53,58,67
GWR workshops 86,*118*,
   119,120
Hall, Dr 67
Hall Walk 44
Harrington, Captain 33
Harris, Salathiel 66
   Mrs S. *101*
Havenor 24
Haymen, John 34
Helston, burgesses of 30
   coinage town 26
Helstone in Trigg 35
Henderson, Charles 16
Hext, Frances M. 11,54
   John 67
   Loveday 55
   Samuel 67
   Thomas 66,*67*
Hexts 51,54,67,75
hill fort, Restormel 12
Hillyar 120

Hood, Sir Samuel 54
Hopton, Sir Ralph 43
Horsebridge 11
Hoskin, Thomas 36
hospital helpers 1939 ..... *107*
Howe, Sir Robert 55
   Lady *110*
Hundred of Powder 11
Hurlers, the 11
Hurrell, Margaret *116*
Ingfangenethof 23,24
Inkepenne, John de 30
inns and hotels
   Byways 74
   Crown & Sceptre 54,74
   Dolphin 74
   Globe 25,54,*113*
   Golden Eagle 74
   Kings Arms' 53,54
   London Inn 74
   Malt Shovel 74
   New Talbot 74
   Royal Oak 76,*100*
   Royal Talbot 76,85,*90*,
                       95,106
   Sailors Arms 74
   Town Arms 73
Iron Age 11,*13*
   mines *69,97*
Italian POWs 89
Jarett, Oscar Henry *96,97*
Javanese sailors *109*
Jeffery, Wilfred 87
Jews' houses 23
John 51,53
   Alexander 53
   John 53
Jones, Gwen Powell 90,*121*
   Thomas 1775 .... *41*
Jordan, Archdeacon 29
Julian's Furniture Shop .. *102*
Kancia, Thomas de 25,51
Kendal 37
   James 53
   Nicholas 1992 51
   Richard 51
   Thomas 51
   Walter 51
   William 51
Kendale, John de ... 30,31,51
Kendals 51,*56*,120
Kerr, Pat MBE 87
Killigrew, John 30
Kings & Queens
   Albert, Prince 73
   Arthur 12
   Athelstan 12
   Charles I 42,51,73
       II 53
   Edward I 24,27
       II 26
       III 26,29
   Elizabeth (1950) *111*
       II 90,*121*
   Gorlois of Cornwall 12
   George VI *111*
   Henry III 18,23,25
      VIII 34,35,*36,38*
   Igraine 12
   Isolda 12
   James I 52
   Mark of Cornwall 12,*13*
   Pendragon, Uther 12
   Richard, Earl of Cornwall
      King of the
         Romans 18,23
         II 33
   Tristan, son of Mark . 12,*13*
   Victoria *72,73,77*
   Wales, Prince & Princess
      of, 1905 .... *96*

William I 15
Knights of the Shire 23
Keast, Ida *121*
Lanhydrock House 43,*59*
Lanlivery 12,24,35,51,66
Lanner 25
Lantyan 12,54
Lanwithan 54,86,88
La Rochelle 16
Launceston 23,24,66
Lawrance, G.B. 3,54
Leavers, Joseph *101*
   Nancy 66
*Leaves from the Journal of
   Our Life in the Highalnds* . 77
Leland, John 36
Lerryn 11
Les Uchel 18
Levant, the 16
Lewes, Battle of 23
Liddicoat, Doris *113,121*
lime kiln *99*
Liskeard 26,44,89
London, William de 24
Looe 11
Lostgwdeyel *21*
Lostwithiel 4,10,*70*
   Assay buildings 24
   Assembly Room 67
   Borough Council 75
   Brass *88* *119*
   Bowls Club 119
   Britain in Bloom 119
   British Legion,
      Women's Section 119
   Brownies 119
   Bypass *107*
   Carnival 119
   Cattle Market (Ltd) . 86,*125*
   Chamber of
      Commerce 90,120
   Christmas Pageant 119
   Coinage Hall 24
   Community Centre
      .... *116*,119
   Conservative Club 119
   Corporation 67
   Cubs 119,*125*
   Exchequer and
      Convocation Hall 24
   Faith Assembly 119
   gaol 120
   Garden Society 119,*124*
   Golf & Country Club .. 119
   Guides *102*,119
   Home Guard 89,*109*
   King George VI
      Playing Field 119
   Luncheon Club 119
   Maps 1642-1880 . *endpapers*
   Market Hall 53,*59*,67
   Mayor's Parlour *121*
   Museum 120
   name 18
   Old Cornwall
      Society 116,120
   Pageant (1989) *122,123*
   Players 120
   Play Group 119
   Pleyber, Christ 119
   Regatta 119
   RNLI 119
   St John Ambulance
      Brigade 119
   Scouts 119
   Silver Band *111*,119
   Silver Seal *41*
   Tourist Information
      Centre 119
   Town Council 119
   W.I. 119

Lostwithoutya 89
Magna Britannia *48*
Malt House *48*
Martelli, Jude 121,*123*
Masonic Hall 75
Matthew, William 68
Maurice, Prince 44
May, Stan *113*
   Victor 88,125
Mayell, F.L. 85
Mayor making 119
medieval market 90
Meet, 1926 .... *103*
Melrose Chronicle 23
Messina 16
milestone 68
milk drying tower *125*
Mock Mayor Choosing . 76,86
Mohun, Sir Wm 51
   Lord 51
Molesworth, Sir John 53
Montfort, Simon de 18
Mortain, Robert Earl of
   Cornwall 15
Muster Rolls, 1569 37
   1588 37
Nanstallon 11
Neal, Miss A.M. *101*
Nelly, Tom *117*
Netherton, Bruce ... 36,*37,41*
   Florence *57*
Nicholls, Charles *91*
   Dorothy de
      Lancey 51,*116*,120
   Dora *101*
   Kate *101*
Nield, James 66
Nomansland *94*
Norden, John 35,36
Norman Conquest 11,16
Norway, A.H. 11,51,54
   Captain 54
   House 54
   Neville 54
Office of Works 36
Old Exchequer Hall 75
Oléron 16
Osborne, Olive *117*
Padstow Workhouse 65
Pageant of History 90
Palace Printers 86,*105*
Panton 25
Par 44
Parker, Derek
   (cartoon) *114*
Pascal, Roger 88
Pearce family 89
Peareth, Stephen *124*
Pelyn House 51,*56,57*
Penknek 18,23,24
Penknight 24,*41*
Penlyne 26
Penquite Farm 86
pewter 34
Pickles, Winifred
   (Have a go) *113*
Pisano, Antonio 26
Pill 88,*109*
Pitt 51,54
   Thomas,
      (Diamond Pitt) 52,57
      of Boconnoc 52
      1st Lord Camelford .. 52
      2nd Lord Camelford . 52
      Robert 52
   William, Earl of
      Chatham 52
Pleyber-Christ *124*
Plymouth 31,43,45,65,
                   66,74,108

Plympton 31
Polhampton, Richard de .. 26
Polkerris *119*
Polruan 16,29,33,44
Pontsmill 11
Poor House 66,68
Pound, Norman 73
postcard 1913 .... *98*
Post Office 73
poster 1822 .... *71*
Priories,
   St Andrews 16,35
   St Sergius & St Bacchus,
      Angers 16
Prisoners of War 89
Ptolemy,
   Map of Britain 18,*20*
quay 25
Quoynt Michael 24
R.A.C. 87
Radnor, Earl of 53
R.A.F. 87,89
Radford, Ralegh 11
railway, broad gauge *80*
   carriage *80*
   Milltown Viaduct *81*
   staff c1900 .... *81*
   station building *80*
   ticket (to Fowey) *113*
Raleigh, Sir Walter 37
Reading room,
   Bridgend 54,*94*
Rede, Stephen le 51
Redmond, Eileen 86
Reformation, the 35
Restormel 29,36
   Borough Council 89
   Castle 11,12,*14*,15,
      18,23,25,*27,28*,30,
      36,*40*,43,45,73,90,*96*
   court of 31
   earthwork 12,*13*
   House 29,54,*57*
   iron mines 67,73
Robartes 43,51,52
   Hon Francis 53
   John, 1st Lord
      Radnor *47*,53
   Richard 1st Lord
      Robartes 52,*58*
   Hon Russell 53
Robert, Brother 30
Roberts, Alice & Grace 65
Rogers, Richard 66
Roman, roads 11
   settlement 11,18
Roundheads 43
Rowe, Ryan 36
*Royal Cornwall
   Gazette* 65,73,74
Royal Mail coach 65
Rundle, Malah 86
St Austell 44,86,88
St Agnes 66
St Blazey 44
St Faith's Convent 75,77
St George's Park 88
St Neot 66
Sake 23,24
Sanchia 25
Santo, Abigail 86
   Esme *116*,120
Saxons 12,15
Schools, Elementary 75
   Bodmin Hill 54,*101,110*
   Commercial 67
   Grammar 1770-1842 ... 53,
                      59,67,87,88
St Winnow 54
Sealed Knot Society *46*
Secombe, Frank 90

Seisons, Caption of 1337 26
Sheriffs 24,29
Shire Hall *22,26,32,39,*
75,86
    Coinage Hall 24
    Convocation Hall 24,*78*
    Exchequer 24
    Stannary gaol 24,25
    Parliament 24
    tynne porch 24
shoot (water) 75,*82*
Shreepur Orphanage 87
Shute, Neville 54
Siege of Lostwithiel 47
Simms, John 66
Skelton, Bill 85
Skelton's Garage ... 87,88,*103*
Skippon, General 45
Slaughterhouse winch *105*
Soke 23,24
Southampton 31
South West Water
    Company 75
Springfields 89
Stamford, Lord 43
Stanniforth, Thomas 67
Stannaries, Warden of 17,
26,33,37
Stannary prison . 24,66,*69*,74
    towns 17,24
Stannators 34
Star, the 66
Stephens, Rex *116*
stewards 24
stocks *70*
Stoke Climsland 35
Stratton 11

Straughan, Col 44
streets, roads & lanes
    Bodmin Hill .. 46,*48*,74,75,
85,87,88,*93,99*
    Bunkers Hill 76
    Castle Hill (Tangier) 66
    Church Lane 24
    Crockerne Street 46
    Duke Street 85,101,105
    Eveleighs Row 67
    Fore Street *3*,24,46,53,
54,*60*,74,87,*92*
    King Street 55,*60*
    Knights Row 67
    Liddicoat Road 88
    Market Street *72*
    Monmouth Square *103*
    Mount Pleasant 46,*48*
    Moors, the 66,74
    Nomansland Hill 85
    North Street .. *32*,46,54,*78*,
82,86,88,*103*
    Parade, The 85
    Philps Court 67
    Queen Street 46,*72*,74,
84,86,87,88,*93*
    Robertes Terrace *108*
    South Street 11,88
    Summer Lane 66
    Tanhouse Lane 46,88
    Terras Hill 46,*60*,66
Strong, Betty *117*
    Walter *117*
Suffrage, universal 1928 .. 87
Sunday Schools 75
    Bank 89
    Wesley 89

Symonds, Richard 44
Talling *82*
    Desmond 88
    Eileen 88
Tamar 43,65
tannery pump *79*
Taprell *39*,51,53
    House 36,*39*,*40*,53,55
    John 53
    Martha 53
    Ralph 51,53
    William 53
Thegn 23,24
Thetherway, Desmond 87
Thol 23,24
tin 15
    coinage 25,*37*,76
    foreign trade 16,17
    miners *70*,77
    stamp *37*
Tintagel 12,23
Titus, Silas MP *33*,41
toll houses *91*,94
Tomlin, family 105
    Odessa 85,89,*101*
Torpoint 65
Tower of London 23
Town lands 51
    Sargeant 66
    quay *99*
Tracy, Isolda de 18,23
    Thomas de 18
Treleaven, Margaret 65
    Peter 65
Trematon 23,30
Tristan Stone *13*
Tristan's woods 12

Truro 26,33,65
Turstin 15
Tywardreath 16
Uzella 18
Vancouver, George 52,*57*
Vane, John 66
vestry book 65
Victoria 97
Villa Regis 33
Vincent, John 97
Wadebridge 25
wagonette 1905 .... *90*
Walkham, Richard 86,*95*
    Kate 86
wars, Boer 85
    Napoleonic 65,66
    1st World 85,*87*
    2nd World 88
Waryson, Peter 35
Watts, Ruby (née Bevis) ... 87
Wengfeld, Sir John 30
West Briton 66,74
Wesley, John 55
Wharf *69*
Wherry, W.J. *105*
Wilce's shop 1906 .... *91*
Williams, Henry 88
    Thomas 65
Winchester Assize Hall
    Returns 17
window tax *49*
Wiseman, Ralph 24
Woen, Melchisedek 46
Wooley, Walter 35
Working Men's Institute .. *82*
W.R.V.S. 120
Young, Denholm 23

Subscribers

Presentation Copies

1 Lostwithiel Town Council
2 Restormel Borough Council
3 Cornwall County Council
4 Lostwithiel Library
5 Cllr A. Warren Nicholls

6 Barbara & Ian Fraser
7 Clive & Carolyn Birch
8 David Owens
9 Church Town Farm Outdoor Educational Centre
10 Fiona Toft
11 Marion Livesley
12 Geoffrey & Kathleen Sharpe
13 Janet Fraser
14 David & Catherine Geddes
15 Stephen & Diane Sharpe
16 Philip & Sarah James
17 Massimo & Mary Beber Fraser
18 Dheeren & Elizabeth Patel
19 Keith & Zoe French
20 L.R. Bachmann
21 C.A. Spinks
22-25 J.E.G. Vivian
26 A.J. Barclay
27 J. Gilbert
28 W.T.B. Doney
29 R.M. Harris
30 Roger Dongray
31 Amanda Sheila Onslow Sands
32 Jean Moore
33 Daphne Bryant
34 J.R. Jeffery
35 Ann Bragg
36 Nigel Williams
37 Mr & Mrs J.F. Rogan
38 Ian Kerr
39 W/Cdr & Mrs H.R. Kerr
40 Patricia Kerr MBE
41 Brian & Susan Grigg
42 Mr & Mrs W.K. Beard
43 Anne Elphick
44 G.S. Henwood
45 W.H. Wheeler
46 P.A. Wheeler
47 F.G. Durrant
48 E.A. Whitworth
49 A.C. Taylor
50 Josephine Taylor
51 S.E. Vague
52 E.R. Collins
53 M.A. Treleaven
54 P.J. Treleaven
55 J.L. Smedley
56 Janet M.W. Allison
57-58 Miss B. Stephens
59 Paul V. Brewer
60 Dawn Goodship
61 D.J. Taylor
62-79 Cornwall County Council
80 Bruce Burley
81 Rev F.R. Sydenham
82 J. Blowey
83 Colin A. Cornish
84 John Hooper
85 F.G. Ramage
86 R.M.F. Oliver
87 Mrs V. Motchman
88 M.J. Martyn
89 M. Thomas
90 H.M.A. Bishop
91 Peter Isbell
92 Michael Trinick
93 John Blowey
94 M.J. Keast
95 Collin W. Brewer
96 Elizabeth Gane
97 John Skelton
98 D.P. Ball
99 Anne Turner
100 R.D. Barbery
101 Rev Brian Coombes
102 F.L. Bulmer
103 Freda S. Tillett
104 Margaret Burgess
105 J.K.J. Burrow
106 J.F. Morgan
107 C.P. Eich
108 Bernard H. Broad
109 I.H. Roberson
110 Mrs P. Woodhouse
111 Derek L. Brown
112 Keith Hamylton Jones
113 G.R. Vaughan Ellis
114 Mr & Mrs M. Wilkins
115 G. Billing
116 Hilary Shaw
117 Royal Institution Of Cornwall
118 Bruce Burley
119 Rosemary Haines
120 Arnold Royston Morgan Bradley
121 David C. Trefery
122 Leonard Hoskins Truran
123 Audrey Williams
124 Elizabeth R. Hutton
125 John Raymond Ward
126 Les & Ruth Baker
127 P.E. Pencheon
128 M.B. Bradby
129 William H. Olford
130 Mr & Mrs L.W. Michell
131 Andrew Foot
132 Miss H.I. Tippet
133 J.D. Jeffery
134 W. John Tonkin
135 H.E. Morton
136 H.H. Madams
137 John Francis Potter
138 Dr & Mrs C.S. Hogg
139 Mr & Mrs P.L. Jones
140 Mrs Lorraine Rolls
141 Dawn Barber
142-143 B.& G. Keast
144 M. Wilkins
145 Sandy Hill School
146 O.E. Jones
147 Mount Charles School
148 R.C.M. Morgan
149 County Libraries
150 Mr & Mrs F.R. Noble
151 Dr Donald Adamson
152 Paul Keast
153 Keith D. Staite
154 Bruce Burley
155 Arnold R.M. Bradley
156 M.T. Anderson
157 Mavis M. Davidson
158 Ivor Thomas
159 Susan Rowe
160 K.M. Brown
161 V.M. Hendy
162 Michael Brown
163 J.S. Russell
164 P. Crago
165 Professor Charles Thomas
166 J.E. Batchelor
167 W.R.V. Crago
168 R.C.R. Saunders
169 Frank Harper
170 John Hooper
171 Mr & Mrs P.O. Bevan
172 Miss K.M. Beard
173 Sylvia Berrill
174 Ingrid V. Bowden
175 Fiona Chisholm
176 W.T.B. Doney
177 Mr & Mrs M.J. Drayton
178 E.C. Gardener
179 J. Gilbert
180 Mr & Mrs M.G. Hine
181 Dawn Hutchings
182 C.J. Jones
183 Mrs McLeod
184 Mary Liddicoat
185 D.J. Partridge
186 John Pegg
187 G. Perry
188 R.W. Phillips
189 Graham Phillips
190 Nigel Poole
191-192 Mrs P.A. Roberts
193 Lilian Rowe
194 Mrs J. Simon
195 Valerie Strout
196 Mr & Mrs D.H. Talling
197 J. Ivor Thomas
198 Mrs L. Turpie
199 John Watts
200 Lisa Webb
201 Mrs Jill Wigley
202 Mr & Mrs Whiffing
203 Alexander Wilton
204 Benjamin Wilton
205 Rev Alf Williams
206 Mrs S.M. Berry
207-208 Martin S. Sands
209 Brian Santo
210 M.T. Anderson
211 Gordon Faddy
212 Myra Hicks
213 Matthew Hedger
214 Nigel & Joan Markwick
215 Peter Francis James
216 D.J. Oakley
217 F.J. Ashton
218 Ann & John Carter
219 Fowey Community School
220 S. Cleaver
221 Joan Smith
222 G.J. Smith
223 A.B. Pearce
224 Ron & Doreen Brown
225 Carey Brown
226 John & Kay Copleston
227 John & Jill Blanchard
228 Bill & Mary Meakin
229 Mr & Mrs Jonathan Barker
230 D.R. Emery
231 John & Margaret Andrew

232 Vera Andrew	252 D.J. & J.H. Dunkley	268 Mrs Renee Keast	326 St Winnow CofE School
233 Mr & Mrs Caffap	253 Eric & Jean Gadd	269- Cornwall County Council	327 Lostwithiel Junior/
234 J.M. Sharman	254 T.H. & M.E. Shimmins	305 Libraries & Arts Dept	Infant School
235 Allen Narbett	255 John Shimmins	306 P. Julian	328 Alistair C. Duguid
236-237 Mrs R. Pearce	256 Margaret Cazaly	307 R.A. Stephens	329 Mrs M. Wilton
	257 M.A. Cooksley	308 J. Brumby	330- Cornwall County Council
238 L. Harris	258 Gwyneth Hambridge	309 C.L. Jewels	347 Libraries & Arts Dept
239 Charles Day	259 Jude Martelli	310 C.A. Woodward	348 Nigel Poole
240 M.T. Perry	260 S. Taperell	311 P.J. Evans	349 Cyril P. Bunn
241 H.A. Liddicoat	261 G. Taperell	312 C.O. Jones	350 Mrs M. Powell
242 Mena Smith	262 Plymouth Museum &	313-316 Margaret Jeffery	351 Mr & Mrs D. Platt
243 Richard Munden Bower	Art Gallery		352 Francis Stephens
244 W. Melville Mitchell	263 The National Trust	317-318 J. Reed	353 Alan Sharpe
245 C. Clemow	264 Captain & Mrs J.D.G.		354 W.J. Martin
246 Margaret T. Lees	Fortescue	319-320 A.J. Wright	355 E.M. Furse
247 Bob & Viv Acton	265 Mr & Mrs Colin Williams		356 R. Pearce
248 J. Crago	266 Mr & Mrs A. Warren	321 Mrs M. Wilton	357 Mavis & Dennis Walford
249 P.J. Evans	Nicholls (Mayor 1993)	322 Peggy & Patrick Chudleigh	358 Fiona Toft
250 C.W. Brewer	267 Mr & Mrs R.F. Edward-	323 Sarah Chudleigh	359 Donald & Janet James
251 P.C. Richards	Collins	324 Stephen Chudleigh	*(remaining names unlisted)*
		325 Elizabeth Chudleigh	

Key to Caption Credits

B&FN	Bruce and Florence Netherton	JDGF	J. Desmond G. Fortescue
BL	British Library	JS&JW	June Stephens and Joy Worden
BM	British Museum	LM	Lostwithiel Museum
CAS	Cornwall Archaeological Society	LSC	Lostwithiel Social Club
CAU	Cornwall Archaeology Unit	LTC	Lostwithiel Town Council
CB	Christine Barnicoat	MES	M. Eileen Shimmins
CD	Charles Day	MH	Margaret Hurrell
CPB	Cyril Bunn	MH&PD	Margaret Hoskins and Pauline Dustow
CRO	Cornwall Records Office	MR	Malah Rundle
CSL	Cornish Studies Library	MW	Margery Worden
DB	Daphne Bryant	NT	National Trust
DCRS	Devon and Cornwall Record Society	RA	Royal Archives, Windsor
D&ET	Desmond and Eileen Talling	R&DB	Ron and Doreen Brown
DL	Doris Liddicoat	RevFS	Rev F. Sydenham
DonB	Don Breckon	RFE-C	Richard F. Edward-Collins
DT	Desmond Trethewey	RIC	Royal Institution of Cornwall
FMH	Frances M. Hext	RK	Rosemary Kerr
GBL	George Bell Lawrance	RR	Ryan Rowe
I&CK	Ian and Carol Kitt	SBC	The Rector and PCC St Bartholomew's Parish Church
IF	Ian Fraser		
JB	Jonathan Barker	V&AM	Victor and Angela May
JB&MO	Jill Blanchard and Michael Olver	WN	Warren Nicholls

ENDPAPERS — FRONT: Cornwall 1642; (IF) BACK: Lostwithiel 1880 OS Map. (CSL)